Cary Grant

# CARY GRANT

A celebration by Richard Schickel

BLOOMSBURY BOOKS

*For Carol*
*who makes the author*
*feel as if he were the subject*

First published in 1983 by
Pavilion Books Limited

This edition published 1995 by
Bloomsbury Books an imprint of
Godfrey Cave Associates
42 Bloomsbury Street
London WC1B 3QJ

ISBN 1-85471-497-X

© 1983 Richard Schickel

Printed and bound in Italy

# CONTENTS

# INTRODUCTION

DESPITE THE VAST ATTENTION THAT HAS BEEN paid to movie stardom over the seventy year life of that institution, despite the endless interviewing and profiling of its exemplars that continues to proceed apace, the process by which a great and enduring star personality is created and sustained in the public eye is one of the least intelligently examined phenomena of popular culture. Mostly critics, journalists and the audience have contented themselves with the faintly contemptuous belief that movie stars 'play themselves'. This has been considered a lesser act of creation than the conventional role playing of the stage – as if one's self does not infuse the interpretation of any role, even the classical ones – and as if playing oneself were easy, when in fact it is the most difficult part anyone can undertake, given the confusing, literally self-contradictory mass of data at hand, and the problems subjectivity imposes on the task of selecting and presenting the self or perhaps more properly *a* self.

'To play your self – your true self – is the hardest thing in the world to do. Watch people at a party. They're playing themselves ... but nine out of ten times the image they adopt of themselves is the wrong one...' The speaker knew whereof he spoke, for the speaker was Cary Grant. His choice of words was significant, suggesting that all of us, screen stars or not, have a large range of selves available to us when we set forth on the path of self-portrayal. We are not realistic novelists after all; we can't put everything in, not even all the good bits. We have to pick and choose among the images within our range, stress one quality now, another then, and hope that over the long run our public, be it large or small, will more or less get the idea of us – and that it will be a pleasant one.

Selectivity always suggests art and, in the case of the very few stars who achieve the magnitude of Cary Grant, art of a very high and subtle order. Indeed, the evidence both of our eyes and of such testimony on the point that the star himself offered, suggests that Grant went further than most in that the screen character he created starting some time in the mid-1930s, drew on almost nothing from his autobiography, was created almost entirely out of his fantasies of what he would like to have been from the start, what he longed to become in the end. He in fact said that he first created an image for himself on the screen, then endeavored to learn to play it off-screen as well as he did on. This is not an unknown phenomenon. Most stars to some degree become what they have played over the course of the years. But the refraction was more intense in Grant's case, and the more interesting therefore.

By this I do not mean to imply that Grant totally eliminated from his screen presence all traces of his humble and troubling childhood. If he had I think he would have had a short and not very merry screen career as a rather vapid juvenile, perhaps, or as a second-string leading man of no great distinction. No, there was always something more there – clouds constantly scudding across what we perhaps erroneously understood as an entirely sunny personality, sometimes quite blotting out its light. It would be too much to suggest that he hinted at tragic dimensions in any of his roles, but there was always a wariness in him, an uneasy sense that the perfect tailoring might at any time become unravelled, whether through comic or melodramatic encounters. And just as he implied a sense that circumstances might not always be what they at first seemed to be, he also implied a feeling that people – and most especially women – were not always what they claimed to be either. The possibilities of inconstancy and duplicity seemed always to be on his mind – even when they were not necessarily on the minds of director and screenwriter. These possibilities did not make him anxious, but they did make him careful, even (it sometimes seemed) a little bit depressed underneath the charm and ease with which he confronted people and events. It was there that

Young man about town: Grant joins a grass-skirted Mary Pickford, the Countess de Frasso and Tullio Carminati at writer Donald Ogden Stewart's costume party at the Vendome, *c.* 1933. Guests were supposed to come dressed as their favorite stars. Just who this group was impersonating is lost in the mists of memory. Among those identifiable on another night on the town are Randolph Scott, Carole Lombard, Regis Toomey, Toby Wing and, of course, the former Archie Leach.

his singularity and his specificity as a character lay; and it was there, finally, that his appeal lay. For it was that hint of a darker knowledgeableness underlying the more confident and seductive forms of knowingness that tugged at the mind and lingered in the memory. And most important humanized him, permitted us our identification with him.

Typically the assumption that a star 'plays himself' justifies the demand for interviews with him, not to mention the general interest the public takes in allegedly intimate anecdotes and gossip about him. For if a man is only playing himself then manifestly the exposure of that self, a probing of its history in search of its unspoken secrets, will reveal the sources of his magical hold on us. This, I have come to believe, is an error of enormous proportions. And it was especially true of someone like Cary Grant who, if he drew on himself at all drew not on his autobiography as such, but on his most elusive feelings, remembered states of mind, which normally lay well beyond the purview of the written word. I do not believe that in an essay of the kind that follows I have the right or the duty (or the knowledge) to pursue such a course. What I have had available to me is the public record he has left – his films and a scattering of what seem to me reliably recorded public statements by and about Grant the actor. From these I have attempted to re-create and interpret his screen character – in other words to make a plausible critical evaluation of one of the most delightful and indelible screen personalities ever to insinuate itself into our collective consciousness – and unconsciousness. This creation has always seemed to me more complex, more elusive, more subtle than most critics – and certainly most gossipists – have ever credited it with being. If, inevitably, I have touched on aspects of Cary Grant's life, I have, by design, made no effort to intrude on his privacy, to go beyond the public record as he preferred to let it stand. My hope is that this essay will enrich the reader's understanding of what he was up to on the screen, demonstrate that there was more at work before our eyes than simple charm.

Richard Schickel

# 1 IMPECCABLE MAGIC

THE FIRST EDITION OF THIS BOOK WAS PREPARED as a tribute to its subject on his eightieth birthday, and one approached the task with due diffidence. The intention of course was to celebrate. What mood or mode other than the celebratory would have been appropriate to such an occasion? For as long as we had known him – and for most of us that had been for the lengths of our lifetimes – he had been the object of, and inspiration for, a delight so innocent and perfect that the attempt to analyse its sources seemed almost an act of ingratitude, a laying on of thumby, even besmirching, hands that would inevitably fumble the job. And possibly earn the scorn of the subject, not to mention the impatience of the reader.

This was a matter on which Grant had for many years been uncharacteristically grouchy. 'When I read about myself, it is so *not* about me that I'm inclined to believe it's really about the writer,' he said in his only autobiographical jottings, a quarter of a century ago. 'Fantasy, exaggeration, drivel, or further embellished retellings of past inaccuracies,' he called the journalism that had accreted around his admirably elusive private self and an image that was more complex as a creation, if not in its final effect, than people liked to think it.

Yes. The usual, and usually justified, complaint of the public figure. And one that bitter experience had taught him cannot be rectified. For he knew that even if he replaced silence with loquaciousness the press, although it might cease to make up things about him, could not escape its own limitations, which included the custom of incompetence, and so would inevitably continue to misapprehend and misquote him. 'Go ahead, I give you permission to misquote me,' Grant once told an interviewer, 'I improve in misquotation.' Maybe so, but one really did hesitate to chance it. If fantasy, exaggeration or drivel here ensue, let it be understood that they arise from an earnest, if cheerful, effort to understand not the man who was born into the world as Archibald Alexander Leach, but that brilliant and utterly essential figure of fantasy which, with a little help from his friends, he created; the figure we knew, or thought we knew, as Cary Grant.

'Man is the only animal that reviews,' said Marshall Brickman, the comedy writer, a little while ago. So as a member of that slightly exotic subspecies, doomed by some grim Darwinian jest to shoulder a seemingly inescapable burden on behalf of the racial need for the critical gesture, one felt that perhaps the best gift one could bring to the anniversary fete was a small sample of one's curious speciality. A humble gift, doubtless, but in at least one sense of the word, a thoughtful one – handmade, toiled over, a labor of love, really. For one does deeply care about the movies and therefore cannot help but agree with an admired colleague, David Thomson, author of one of the two worthwhile essays on Cary Grant, that it is simply impossible to think about movies without him, a statement difficult to make about any other star this side of James Cagney.

But the moment one picked up one's critical tatting and began to contemplate its design, a daunting thought occurred. It was that the very occasion that inspired it – Cary Grant's passage to octagenarian status – struck one as improbable, impossible to accept. People would say: 'Cary Grant – eighty? You've got to be kidding.' For something singular, something entirely without precedent in movie history, in any kind of history, for that matter, happened in the life of Cary Grant, therefore in our perception of him. That is, very simply, that some time in his fifties, while he still looked as if he were in his forties – happily combining an elegant and easeful maturity with an undiminished capacity for playfulness – he simply ceased to age. Just plain stopped. As far as we in the audience could see. As far as his intimates could see, too. 'Everyone grows older,' his friend and co-star Grace Kelly (twenty-four years his junior) once conceded wearily, 'except Cary Grant.'

Mae West's once and future co-stars, W. C. Fields and Grant, join friends at a Hollywood jolly up in 1933. At right, Grant ran into Marlene Dietrich, his *Blonde Venus* co-star on a 1938 crossing of the *Normandie*, and they posed for ship's news photographers when the ship docked in New York 'just in time for Thanksgiving dinner' as the wire service caption put it. Somehow, one does not think of either of them gnawing on a drumstick with much enthusiasm.

It was uncanny. Many of his contemporaries clung to their careers, and in a certain sense clung to their looks, which is to say that they aged gracefully, more gracefully (thanks to artful cameramen and even more artful plastic surgeons) than ordinary mortals did. But they did so at the price of denaturing themselves or, at least, their former screen selves. They played grizzled westerners, or befuddled sitcom daddies or elder statesmen, pillars of this community or that. But they did not get the girl. If a woman was placed anywhere near them she was not a girl and usually they already had her – some nice plain Jane wife-type, with whom one imagines them comfortably playing gin rummy as they declined into an impotence about which she was good-natured. But not Cary Grant. Cary Grant had rarely chased girls anyway – they had more often chased him – and they were permitted to go right on doing so, in approximately the same context they had always done, that is in romantic comedies. These were not as good as they once had been, but they were their star's natural milieu. And since their most obvious conventions, though not their true spirit, were as they had ever been, they helped to keep Grant's screen persona isolated from such contemporary realities as might contrast too vividly with it, jar us from the pleasant time capsule in which he had encased himself. Such was the persuasiveness of his charm and the good nature of his vehicles, they did not engender, in and of themselves, many stray thoughts about how time seemed to be fleeing for everyone but Cary Grant. One rarely stopped to think that he alone among our institutions refused to acknowledge such unpleasantness as the Cold War (which was remarkable considering that two of his best late films involved espionage), changing sexual mores (which was even more remarkable, considering that virtually all of those late films involved romantic contretemps of some sort) or the general fall-off of manners, dress and, for that matter, interior decoration.

The last significant historical occurrence in his realm was the Second World War; everything that occurred thereafter, including Holiday Inns, fast food and even television went determinedly unacknowledged. He still travelled by boat, dressed for dinner, and was never inconvenienced by the decline of the serving class.

Grant never acknowledged any conscious strategy in the selection of these vehicles, which more often than not he produced himself. Pressed on the point he took a view one could well have imagine one of his screen characters expressing. 'Life is to be enjoyed ... If I didn't like making comedies, I wouldn't make them. I certainly don't *have* to.' No more did he take any extraordinary credit for the luck of the genetic draw that seemed to be the largest factor in permitting him to retain his youthful air. He would allow that he sensibly practised moderation in all things, but no Spartan regimens, either dietary or athletic, were ever mentioned. In the late 1950s and early 1960s, it is true, he went determinedly public with the news that he had experimented with a carefully

controlled program that involved a combination of LSD and psychiatric therapy. To this he attributed, in his word, a 'rebirth', and implied that his continuing youthfulness of manner and appearance might well be one of the boons he derived from it. But since he had looked fine before embarking on that program, and continued in his splendidness well after he had left it, one was inclined to discount his claims for its physical fringe benefits, however well it made him feel in other respects, and however serious he was in his belief that hallucinogenics, properly prescribed and monitored, might have significant psychiatric uses.

But if he was peculiarly blessed in his resistance to the visible manifestations of the aging process, that did not mean he was immune to the professional benefits to be derived from his good fortune and he shrewdly capitalised on them. His strategy was to play down the age question when it was raised, which it generally was when the press doltishly appeared, looking as always for 'an angle'. For a time he professed honest puzzlement on the point. He said that

the birth records of the city of Bristol, England, where he was born, had been destroyed in a wartime bombing raid and so he could not satisfy even his own curiosity on the matter of his birth date, conveniently ignoring the fact that his vital statistics, like those of all other Englishmen, are kept centrally in London, and that these records were spared by the bombers. Sometimes he could be disarmingly funny about the question. In the famous exchange of telegrams that one devoutly hopes is not apocryphal, the query from the magazine arrived reading: HOW OLD CARY GRANT? And the reply went forth: OLD CARY GRANT FINE. HOW YOU? Often though, he became uncharacteristically cranky on the subject: 'I'm sick and tired of being questioned about why I look young for my age and why I keep trim,' he told a reporter in 1960. 'Why should people make so much of it? Why don't they emulate it rather than gasp about it?' Whereupon he launched into a tirade about smoking, the imbibing of 'poisonous liquids', the use of greasy, pore-clogging make-up. These unfortunate habits, he said, so debilitated their addicts that they were rendered incapable of doing the one thing they should be doing – making love.

Most unusual, an outburst of that sort. But perhaps a measure of how significant the appearance of agelessness, however accidental its causes, had become to him. And, as he obviously understood, to the rest of us. For Cary Grant – no, better to write it thus, 'Cary Grant' – was, is, and always has been, a pure fantasy creation, far purer than any other star creation one can think of. Among the few contemporaries who were his peers something of their autobiographies, something of the time and place that had made them, whether it was Cagney's New York or Fonda's Nebraska, clung to them, was a presence in their presences. These hints of truth are what grounded their screen characters in reality, granted believability to whatever outrageously improbable behaviour – heroic or comic or romantic – the script called upon them to perform. Besides specificity it gave them singularity as well. It is what made them stand out from their competitors, made them memorable even when many of their roles were not. With Grant it was, as we will have occasion to observe in more detail, quite the opposite. The persona he constructed deliberately referred to nothing in his life or in the life of his times. Mostly he played not what he had been, but what as a youth, he wished he could be, not a remembered reality, but a remembered dream. His screen character was a stylisation, based on previous stylisations that he had observed around show business, and although he became a nominal star within a couple years after his first screen appearance, he did not become one in the fullest meaning of the term until several years later, when the movies themselves evolved a highly stylised conceit, the lunatic 1930's comedy which could encompass this creation of his, give it the proper setting as it were. Looking back, one sees that the only great star of his era who truly offers an analogy with Grant is that other great purveyor of highly stylised stylishness, Fred Astaire, who like Grant offered no hint of personal history on screen, and had to wait for, and help to form, an imaginative world in which his great creation could breathe easily and live naturally. To put it as simply as possible, they were the only men in screen history, in the history of this century, who looked as if they belonged in top hat and tails.

All of this being so, the fact that Grant's creation now appeared to be, in the 1950s and 1960s, after such a long and carefree time before the public, resistant to the pull of the years, to mortality itself, became for its creator a sort of unearned increment on his long, effortless-seeming effort at self-creation, a perfect, unsought, previously unimagined climax to his life's work. Having been for so many years so near magically impeccable in looks, in dress, in manner, in his comic and romantic

timing, now – could it have been otherwise? – he was blessed with this final impeccability. And make no mistake about it, it is precisely impeccability, or anyway, one's last hope of attaining it, that age takes from us.

But not *from* him. And so not *for* him age's dull messiness – the blurring of jawline and waistline, the dimming of eyes and of memory; not for him the inconvenience and degradation of chronic illness or the slow but inexorable dwindling of powers, mental, physical, sexual, that are the doom the rest of us share. He once said to a journalist that when he was young he had never worried about death because he had assumed that science would take care of that problem before he would be required to deal with it. That much good fortune was obviously not to be his. But the next best thing was. And so he would proceed blithely on, until he found himself one day playing a man who did *not* get the girl (in 1967, in *Walk, Don't Run*). He was a good sport about it, telling the press that any other outcome would be tasteless considering his years, but it clearly did not suit him. Cary Grant was no longer 'Cary Grant'.

And so he ceased finally to be him. And became the rather ghostly figure he has become, the grey-haired figure the cameramen occasionally catch at the airport or dining out with friends who, though wealthy and favored, seem rather staid – as befits the 'businessman' that he now styles himself as being. There are no memoirs, no confessions, and he insists there will not be. To write them, he has said, 'you've got to expose other people and I hope to get out of this world as gracefully as possible, without embarrassing them or me...' Which is a nice, Cary Grantish thought. In short, having created 'Cary Grant' out of a cloth as whole as that out of which Walt Disney created Mickey Mouse, he felt entirely free to dispense with him, erase him as it were. And in much the same manner that he had created him, that is to say in a subtle and seemly and slightly mysterious manner, without shock to his or to

14

anyone else's nervous system, without regrets and without undignified appeals to sentiment.

But he created a problem for his would-be analyst. For the length of his unacknowledged autumn was very long – roughly two decades – and though it contained one of his quintessential roles, and at least a couple of good ones, the fact is that the interaction between star and chosen genre became in those years unbalanced, one-sided. In his peak years, just before the outbreak of the Second World War, that relationship had been mutually enlivening. For the craftsmen who had worked with him in the films that we think of both as his classics and the classics of the genre, had been inventive to the point of lunacy, and they had kept putting him in situations that called for an answering inventiveness, an answering lunacy from him. After the war, though, the conventions that had sustained him and the kind of pictures in which he was at his best, that is to say his freest, no longer worked. Comedy like everything else in American life was declassed. Rich and poor alike – and both had been essential to screwball comedy – aspired now, both on screen and off, to bourgeois status. The effect on Grant in particular (and on comedy in general, it must be said), was to cut off his top range – his giddiness, the wondrous ease with which he slipped from elegance to fall-down farcicality – and (to a lesser extent) his bottom range – those enigmatic silences of his, that watchful waiting, half-amused, half-wary, but with more than a hint of both misanthropy and misogeny. He was left, of course, with his middle range, that is to say with his much-discussed charm, his never-overbearing sophistication, his adorability, if you

will. We were comfortable with all that, and these are, surely qualities that are rare and never wear out their welcome. But if one agrees with David Thomson that we are discussing here 'the best and most important actor in the history of the cinema' (even if one only half agrees, or agrees merely for the sake of argument) the case cannot be proved from these late films. Indeed, it is impossible to determine from them what it was about him that originally arrested everyone's attention, what it was that made him a star in the first place and conferred on him the power that enabled him to become the other things he had wanted to be, the 'actor-manager' (a type he had known and admired in his youthful trouping days) who so cleverly sustained himself against the odds that postwar America posted against him. Above all, based on these films alone it is impossible to explain to people born after, say, 1940, what he means to some of us who grew up in his inescapable presence, what richnesses and mysteries, what fascinations were to be found in it.

Not long ago a pair of screenwriters were talking to a young television executive about an idea for a comedy they had. The youth was bright and amiable and eager to get their point, despite some difficulties with it. Finally, however, a light dawned: 'Oh, I get it – Cary Grant in *An Affair to Remember*,' he said. No, they both wanted to cry, Cary Grant in *The Awful Truth*. Cary Grant in *Holiday*. Even Cary Grant in *Mr Lucky* or *In Name Only*. Instead, wanting to make the sale, they nodded, settling for the half truth, the much less funny and ambiguous and even suspenseful truth, not for the truth to which we aspire here.

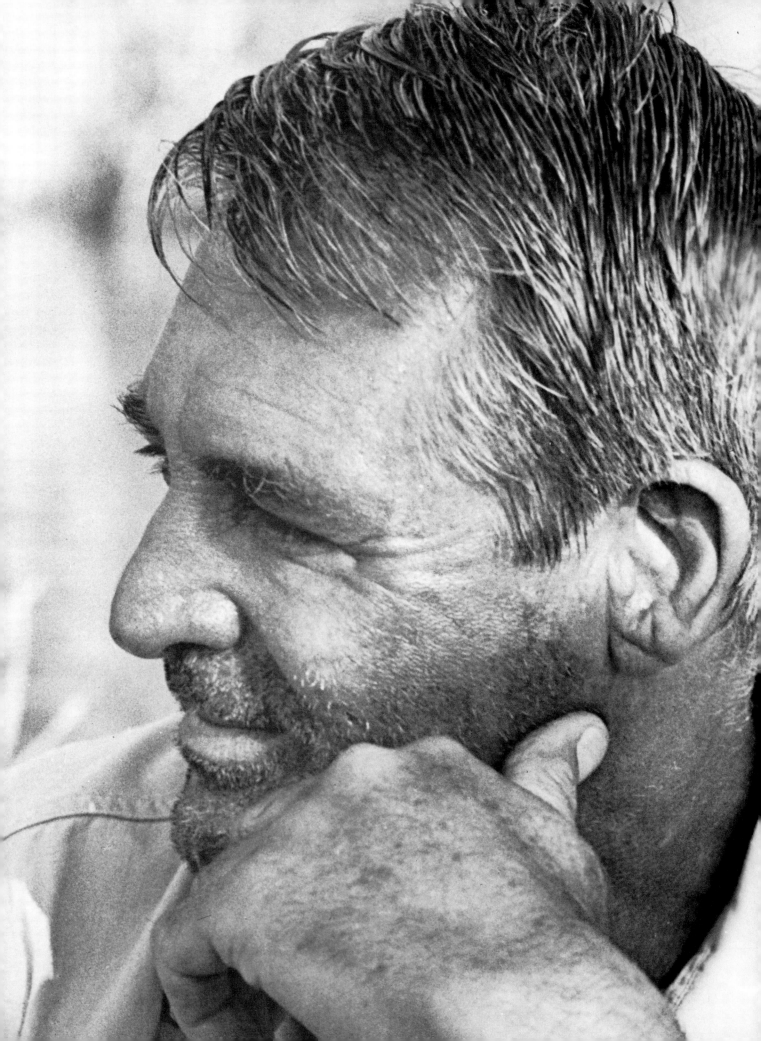

# 2 DARKNESS INTO LIGHT

THE REASON DAVID THOMSON THOUGHT SO highly of Cary Grant as an actor was that 'He can be attractive and unattractive simultaneously; there is a bright side and a dark side to him, but whichever is dominant, the other creeps into view.' This is a reading of his screen character that will startle and doubtless dismay many people, so much have we now staked on the immutability of his charm out of our need for it in a blunt and clumsy world. But obviously I think Thomson is correct; there would be small need for, and less pleasure in writing, an essay in praise of a quality that is usually no more than a compound of good looks, pleasant conversation, decent manners and the ability to wear clothes. Indeed, I feel that if all Grant had to offer was something as simple, if as rare, as that, he would now be little more than a pleasant faded memory, like, say, Joel McCrea or Fred MacMurray or Ronald Reagan, unworthy of any lengthy attention at this late date.

Thomson speculates that this alternation, or ambiguity, in Grant's fundamental screen character derives from something basic in the actor's nature, and about that there can be no doubt. For public purposes he may have sloughed off his autobiography along with his accent, but the sense of the world's bleakness, and of human inconstancy, which he could not have helped but acquire in his formative years – that was not easily shrugged off – and never completely so. Thomson's view is that this was 'transmitted to the screen thanks to a rare willingness to commit himself to the camera without fraud, disguise or exaggeration,' but about that one cannot be quite so certain. This seeming artlessness may only have been a lack of art, a lack of canniness and reserve quite understandable in a young man eager to please, eager to get on in the world, and without the resources of duplicity that experience in acting teaches and power permits one finally to deploy. But we are getting ahead of ourselves . . .

'A bright side and a dark side' ... 'psychobiography' is a form of psychobabble, a neologism that looks on the page almost as ugly as it sounds to the ear. Its inelegance belongs nowhere near our elegant hero. But yet the barest recital of what little has been let slip about Archie Leach's childhood leads us, apologising as we go, towards this dismal discipline, not because one wishes to intrude on the well-guarded privacy of Cary Grant, the celebrity, but for what it seems to suggest about the sources of the singular screen character he created, which is not only public property, but now part of just about everyone's mental furnishings.

Archie Leach was born in Bristol, England on 18 January, 1904, the only child of Elias James Leach and Elsie Kingdon (often given as Kingdom) Leach. The father was part-Jewish, but anglicised, and a Mason as well. He was handsome in an almost dashing way, 'blithe' in outward manner, and as a young man, fond of singing – especially music-hall songs – and of his convivial pint with his cronies. But there was, his son was to recall, 'an inward sadness' about him. He worked as a presser for a garment manufacturer, and was never able to rise above that level, a fact that contributed greatly to the unremitting tension in the Leach household. Elsie Leach's family was, like her husband's, lower middle class, but, one gathers, generally more aspiring than his relatives were. She wished her child to show the world signs that his mother knew what was proper and genteel: and he would be kept in baby dresses and, later, in short pants well past their usual times. Curls, too, clung to him longer than he would have liked. Later, he would have piano lessons and he would be sent to a private preparatory school in Bristol, a rather grim-looking Victorian pile that operated as a day school, but which even with the aid of a scholarship strained the Leachs' resources.

The childhood was not Dickensian, or even

Chaplinesque – to make the obvious comparison with another star whose need to escape a dismal youth motivated his creation of a highly stylised screen character, and whose route to it was quite like the one Grant eventually chose. No, the boyhood was more Orwellian than anything else. Reading about Grant's beginnings one thinks of the writer's reminiscences and fictions about a similarly cramped background, a world of small hopes, mean spirits and the desperate struggle to keep up the facade of respectability.

There was almost always a chill in the air – literally so. It seemed to cling to the walls of the succession of stone terraced houses where Archie spent his first years; the small fireplaces in the bedrooms could never seem to dissipate it. 'Ever since,' Grant would later write, 'I've arranged to spend every possible moment where the sun shines warmest.' But the cold was more than a physical fact of life; it was metaphysical as well. Of his parents' large families he would write, 'Few of them, as far as I could appreciate, glowed with the joy of life.' Of his mother and father he would recall mainly 'regular sessions of reproach', as Elsie condemned Elias for his failure to provide a better livelihood, 'against which my father resignedly learned the futility of trying to defend himself'. Grant would say that he incorporated these battles inside his own character, but he was never more specific than that. Perhaps we can speculate that the passivity of his response to the pursuing female in his screen roles, even when that pursuit was far more benign than Elsie Leach's deadly pursuit of her husband, was learned at his father's knee. Perhaps the care he has always taken in interviews not to criticise his former wives, to insist on the point that they all left him, that he never deserted them, stems from the same source, along with the pride he has exhibited in the fact that with three of them he remained on the friendliest of terms after the divorces. Peace at any price – that was Elias' policy where women

were concerned and it appears to have been Grant's.

He has, however, let a more bitter sense of the opposite sex slip once or twice. He would blandly write that he supposed his parents 'did the best they could to prepare me for life, according to the limits of their knowledge' – not in itself the most cordial endorsement for mily man: It is said that Grant met his first wife, rginia Cherill, in the studio commissary. A 'socialite' the press liked to style her) she had been discovered for ns just as accidentally by Charles Chaplin, who spotted r at a boxing match and cast her as the blind girl beloved his Little Fellow in 1931's *City Lights*. She announced r retirement from the screen when she married Grant in 34, and they posed agreeably enough over fence and ckgammon board. But it seems doubtful that they were ever 'very happy' as the original caption for the snap of them returning home from their 1934 wedding trip had it. The picture he was making at the time had an appropriate title – *Thirty Day Princess* – for they separated after a little more than a year. Grant waited until 1942 before claiming his second princess, the much better known and more wealthy 'socialite', Barbara Hutton. They were married (far right) in his garden, and were divorced three years later.

A shipboard meeting (in 1947, on the *Queen Mary*) blossomed into Grant's longest marriage. He and Betsy Drake were wed in 1949 (with Howard Hughes serving as best man). She played opposite him twice and with him, as the photos (below and right) proved in many a pleasant clime. A serious-minded young woman, Grant credited her with turning his attention to psychology and even to consciousness expanding drugs, but they divorced in 1962. His marriage to Dyan Cannon (below, center) was briefer and stormier, but she gave him the child, Jennifer, (opposite, top) for whom he had long yearned. His last wife was Barbara Harris (opposite bottom).

their efforts – but a few paragraphs later he would say that photographs of his mother, 'frail and feminine', did not do justice to 'the extent of her strength, and her will to control.' Many years later – when he was seventy-three, in fact – and engaged in the only squabble with a woman that the public heard vivid hints about (it was with his fourth wife, Dyan Cannon, and involved his rights to visit his daughter) he suddenly exploded: 'Once the female has used the male for procreation, she turns on him and literally devours him.' The metaphor, of course, is drawn from the realm of insect behavior, but one cannot quite avoid the suspicion that the first and most impressive act of this kind that Grant observed at first hand was Elsie's treatment of Elias when Archie Leach was young and impressionable.

And then, without so much as a by your leave, she deserted Elias – and deserted Archie, too. It was extraordinary melodramatic: one day when he was nine years old, Archie came home from school and found that his mother was not there to greet him. She would never be there again. He was for a time given to understand that she had gone to a seaside resort for a rest and would return soon. But she did not and he quickly learned not to question her whereabouts. He would be, apparently, a grown man before discovering where she had gone: to a mental institution; from which she would not return for decades. 'I was not to see my mother again for more than twenty years,' he was to write, 'by which time my name was changed and I was a full-grown man living in America, thousands of miles away in California. I was known to most people of the world by sight and by name, yet not to my mother.'

By any of the standards psychology applies to an event of this kind, this was a trauma. And yet, it would seem, Archie Leach refused to understand it as such, or let it be treated as such. In a repressed family, in a provincial English city in 1913, when people did not openly discuss such matters, that would have been comparatively easy to do. Some cousins moved in with them, and after that Archie and Elias moved in with Archie's paternal grandmother, but more as boarders than as relatives requiring love and care. Just as the moment when Archie learned his mother's actual whereabouts is unclear from the published record, so also it is unclear who was responsible for her commitment, or its long continuance. But in recounting the incident, Grant implies that at least initially, her institutionalisation was voluntary, and that it might be interpreted as a radical method of attaining a marital separation. It is possible, though surely a twenty year incarceration was not part of her plan. But the significant point for our purposes is not what actually happened, but what Archie Leach thought had happened. And what he thought had happened was that his mother had deserted him.

From an episode of this kind an impressionable child – and Archie was surely that – is bound to learn certain hard lessons, and the ones Archie took away from it are hardly unknown or even uncommon. He had already determined from his mother's behavior with his father that women could be wilful and destructive to the male. Now he learned that among the strategies of that wilfulness was the capacity to abandon the male, leaving him to shift shiftlessly for himself. One need scarcely look further for the sources of that unease and reserve that he exhibited around women in most of his screen roles, qualities that often spilled over into the exasperation that was his comic trademark, and which, considering its sources, must be regarded as a little masterpiece of displaced feeling and disguised statement. That a man who had good Freudian reasons to fear and distrust women, to want to avoid their clutches, should become for so many of them the object of their most profound romantic longings precisely because he was intriguingly elusive, so often determined to

escape entanglement with them, may be regarded as a joke bordering upon the cosmic in its proportions.

Not that little Archie could see any of that coming. No, his need for escape was, in late childhood and early adolescence, quite general, but no less poignant for its lack of specific focus. His father provided a model of sorts. He seems simply to have absented himself from the boy's life. There was no open breach, certainly no overt cruelty – just a vague, gentle drifting away. They left the house at different times – he for work, Archie for the school – and they returned at different times. Neither his grandmother nor any other relative stepped forward to fill the emotional empty space, and Archie Leach became what we would now call a latchkey child, capable of making his own meals and generally taking care of himself, though his appearance was often scruffy – buttons missing, the rips in his trousers unmended.

He seems to have formed no close attachments at school or in the boy scout troop that he joined, and he would say that he was always painfully shy around girls. Like so many lonely lads he found that a way of calling attention to himself, even if it was negative attention, was through prankishness. He would in later years be best remembered among his schoolmates as the boy who was constantly being sent to the headmaster – for telling jokes, making wisecracks, using a slingshot in class. He would himself recall being expelled for a short while for trying to peek into the girls' lavatory, though he recalled the act of expulsion as being more vividly and humiliatingly ceremonial than others who remembered the incident did. No one remembers him turning out for school theatricals, or seemingly to take more than an ordinary interest in visiting the cinema, though he would himself declare that his Saturday afternoon glimpses of Chaplin, the Keystone Cops, whatever was playing were the high points of his week. Similarly, he would remember, from earlier years, having a magic lantern

**The Bob Pender Troupe in action. (see page 28)**

contraption and putting on little shows with it, while his father ran the machine. On the whole though, it would seem that a larger, more definitive break was required than a couple of hours of fantasy could provide. And that very early on he reached an understanding of this need. 'I was so often alone and unsettled at home' he would say, so he actively sought out some useful activity – preferably something that would get him away from Bristol for a while.

The outbreak of war offered him his opportunity, a brief taste of how freedom could be put to good use. On a school holiday he joined some other boy scouts working as messengers and guides on the Southampton docks, staging area for the British Expeditionary Force fighting in France. It was a poignant experience for him – the moment of apprehension he saw on the Tommies' faces when he passed out life belts and gave them instructions on their use, the poignancy of posting for them the last let-

ters they would write to their loved ones from native soil, the sight of men wounded previously – some had lost an arm or a leg – going back to serve in some capacity or other. Above all there was the curious, emotionally pungent mixture of apprehension and exhilaration that seemed to permeate this place – rather theatrical if one stops to think of it – that remained for him a vivid, lifelong memory.

When he returned to Bristol he was gripped with a mild case of sea fever. In those days the steamers could make their way from the harbor, via the Avon River, to the center of town, and Grant would watch their comings and goings longingly. Once he says, he even applied for a job as a cabin boy. But 'destiny' – a word of his choosing – had other claims on him. And so accidental was its method of exerting that claim that one is half inclined to think that perhaps some force other than his own will was indeed working on him.

In his list of favorite school courses, which included geography, history and art, chemistry is the odd entry. Perhaps it was the magical and transforming aspects of the experiments that worked on his imagination. At any rate, Archie Leach took to hanging about the lab on rainy afternoons after school, asking questions of a jovial, friendly man whose attitudes towards his numerous family were the direct opposite of Elias Leach's. He found it natural to take a kindly interest in a bright, well-set-up boy who was obviously hungry for companionship. This unnamed benefactor was a part-time assistant brought in to help run the experiments, and he was also an electrician working at the Hippodrome, Bristol's newest variety theater, which had opened in 1912. A fully electrified theater was still something of a novelty in those days, and he offered to show Archie around the house which he had helped to wire.

Archie dropped by the theater on a Saturday, while the matinée was running, and backstage found himself in a realm such as he had never known or imagined before, 'a dazzling

25

Leading man. Elegance did not attend every moment of Grant's career, fond memories and prevailing impression to the contrary notwithstanding. On these pages, a sampling of various confusions and contretemps. Below, with Frances Farmer in *The Toast of New York* (1937) and with Rita Hayworth in *Only Angels Have Wings* (1939). Right, he was his classically elusive bachelor self opposite Betsy Drake in *Every Girl Should Be Married* (1948). Need one add that the picture is posed?

'I just went gay.' So he cried to May Robson, Leona Robert and screwball comedy's inevitable terrier in *Bringing Up Baby* (1938), left. Above, he went dour opposite Ethel Barrymore in 1944's *None But the Lonely Heart*. *The Amazing Quest of Ernest Bliss* (1937) was released under a variety of titles, none of which helped it commercially. The helpful lady is Buena Bent.

land of smiling, jostling people wearing and not wearing all sorts of costumes and doing all sorts of clever things'. Immediately he knew that this was where he belonged. 'What other life could there *be* but that of an actor? They happily travelled and toured. They were classless, cheerful and carefree. They gaily laughed, lived and loved.' Or so it seemed to him, stepping out of the darkness into the light.

It sometimes seems possible that there would be no show business if there were no unhappy homes, no children who desperately needed that circle of warmth and light, that sense of being a near-family that a theatrical company can generate – not to mention the instant gratification of applause, which so many actors understand as an expression of love. Surely the percentage of people whose backgrounds contain at least one parent who is either physically or emotionally absent (and in Grant's case there was one of each) is far higher in the theatrical enterprise than it is in any other occupation. At any rate the homeless boy, now thirteen, had found a home. Or, as he was to put it, 'I had a place to be. And people let me *be* there.'

His mentor got him a non-paying job aiding the electricians who worked the arc lamps (or limelights) at a rival music hall, the Empire, where for some weeks he happily risked burned fingers helping to change and adjust the carbon arcs, an occupation that came to an abrupt end when, working the follow spot from the booth in the front of the house, he accidentally misdirected its beam, revealing that one of an illusionist's best effects was done with mirrors (as, to this day, most of them are). He thereupon beat a retreat back to the Hippodrome, where he made himself useful, as a general errand boy, working backstage.

It was there that he heard that a troupe of boy acrobats, managed by one Bob Pender, was regularly being depleted as the performers reached military age, which was sixteen. Archie Leach was not quite at school-leaving age,

which was fourteen, but he wrote a letter to Pender, in his father's name, offering his services and enclosing a picture that showed a chap tall for his age and well-built, someone who could easily pass for older than his years. Pender replied favorably, telling Archie to report to Norwich for a tryout, and even enclosing rail fare. Archie stole away in the middle of the night, caught the train, and was placed in training with the troupe. It took his father a week to find him, but whatever anger he felt over the incident was disarmed by the agreeable and responsible Pender who, with his wife, ran his company with a due regard for the proprieties. Besides which, he was a Mason, which reassured Elias Leach. They agreed that Archie could return to the troupe as soon as he could legally leave school, an event Grant would later claim he tried to hasten by getting himself expelled for cutting classes and general bad behavior. Whatever the case, he was soon back with Pender, and soon working on stage with the rest of the boys.

Dancing, tumbling, even stilt-walking became part of his repertoire. And above all mime, the ability to convey mood and meaning without resort to dialogue, which was to be so much a part of his genius as a film actor. But for fourteen year old Archie Leach it was the life of the company off stage that was significant, the camaraderie of it. When they were not on tour, or when they were playing one of the London variety circuits, the lads lived, dormitory-style, in the Penders' house in Brixton, in the southeast of the capital, an area that provided digs for performers by the hundreds, since it was handy both to the great city and to the many theaters of the south coast. There was training in the morning, and the boys were expected to help with communal chores, the cooking, cleaning and washing up, before going to work. The hours were regular – breakfast every morning at 7:30, lights out every night at 10 – the structure of his days firmer than he had ever known, and he thrived on

that. There was no room in this group for egotism, for they were together constantly, and, of course, given the kind of work they did, mutual dependency, mutual trust, was a necessity. That sense of Cary Grant as a trouper, as a man who took direction well, did not exert himself to assert himself at the expense of others, on the set or in a scene, which one gathers from the reminiscences of his co-workers later on, has its sources here. He could work easily with just about anyone, and he was always generous in his willingness to exchange roles, for example. Or to give writers their first chance to direct (Clifford Odets, Delmer Daves and Richard Brooks all made that move with Grant's support). In other words, besides implanting the best (and rarest) show business values, Bob Pender and his company in effect civilised the loner and the one-time show-off, gave him what he had been inarticulately, unknowingly seeking. That 'place to be' that he had been looking for was not a place merely to be himself, but a place to be a better self than he had been.

In the process he lost the one thing that might most easily have betrayed his origins – his accent. About this he has never spoken, but since no expert has ever detected anything of the West Country in his tones and everyone can hear in them a touch of what is generally, if erroneously, referred to as Cockney (and more than a mere touch of it when occasions like *Sylvia Scarlett, Gunga Din,* or *None But the Lonely Heart* warrant it) we may assume that he began the process of vocal restyling in these days. For this level of English theatrical life recruited many of its members from lower class London, and took many of its mannerisms from it, too. He did not aim, however, for affectation or pretence, for there is nothing of Oxbridge in his voice either. Better, perhaps, to say that he was striving for something unplaceable, even perhaps untraceable – so much so that some of the people he later hung out with, when he was an actor in New York, called him Kangaroo or Boomerang, thinking perhaps he was an Australian. What he achieved, of course, was singular – an impressionist's delight – but also something that turned out to be remarkably useful, in that he could pass equally well for an Englishman or an American in his screen roles, and could move comfortably up and down the social scale in them as well. There was always a democratic touch of common humanity in his playboys, a touch of natural good breeding in his more raffish roles.

Was he beginning to think about acting? Probably not. For the moment he was content to be free of his past – its constraints and its emptiness. He would recall returning to Bristol for an engagement with the Pender troupe a few months after joining it, and his pleasure in performing before relatives and friends. He stayed with his father that week and he would remember walking home with him after the last performance on the opening through the quiet streets on a summer's night. 'We hardly spoke but I felt so proud of his pleasure and so much pleasure in his pride. And I happily remember that we held hands for part of that walk.'

After that, though, they lost touch. There is no evidence that he returned to Bristol until he had become a star, by which time his father had died, of what was officially described as 'acute toxicity', but which Grant diagnosed as a broken heart, because he had achieved so little of what he had wanted, and was surely, at the bottom line, alcoholism. As of 1920, however, Archie Leach already had more of what he wanted than he had ever dreamed of possessing. His salary with the Pender troupe was only a pound a week (worth about five dollars in those days) over and above room and board, but the life continued good and the act was gaining an excellent reputation – so much so that Charles Dillingham, the American impresario, engaged them.

They sailed for New York on the *Olympic*, among whose passengers were Douglas Fairbanks and Mary Pickford, returning from their European wedding trip, and young Archie was suitably impressed when he found himself playing shuffleboard with Fairbanks and having his picture taken in his company. He found Fairbanks 'affable and warmed by success and well-being, a gentleman in the true sense of the word ... It suddenly dawns on me as this is being written that I've doggedly striven to keep tanned ever since, only because of a desire to emulate his healthful appearance.' As Pauline Kael observes (in the other worthwhile essay about Grant) there was much that Grant shared with Fairbanks besides acrobatic skill – their half-Jewish and alcoholic fathers, for instance, the ease with which both men, in their maturity, moved through widely divergent social circles, their continuing emphasis on fitness. Ultimately, as Kael puts it, 'They were loved by the public in similar ways – for their strapping health and high spirits, for being *on* [her italics] and giving out when they were in front of an audience, for grinning with pleasure at their own good luck.'

He was never precisely an heir to Fairbanks (no one was; he was as singular in his way as Grant was in his), but it does seem significant that on his way to the Land of Opportunity he encountered the impressive man who at the time symbolised to his countrymen and (as the mob scenes he and Mary had just endured proved) to the world at large, something of what was best in its spirit – exuberance, self-confidence, a cheeky good cheer and an almost adolescent nerviness in adversity. For a man coming out of darkness into light, there was, possibly, a promise in Fairbanks. If other Americans were like him, then the chill that had been bred in Archie Leach's bones might finally be drawn out of him.

New York offered further hope in that regard. It was, in those days, when the splendid Woolworth Building was still its – and the world's – tallest structure, a shining city, bustling, yet civilised, and certainly among the young people – experimenting with new forms in the traditional culture, or exploring the possibilities of melding that culture with a popular culture newly animated by technological innovation – as classless as any one might wish. Archie Leach, now sixteen, would take it all in, wide-eyed, mostly silent, always polite, when he was riding the open top of a Fifth Avenue bus the length of the avenue or, a little later, sitting with the bright young men at Rudley's cafeteria on 41st and Broadway – among them were Moss Hart and Preston Sturges – who were full of enthusiasm for a new theater. He would eventually get to know the Algonquin crowd too, and, as a handsome and mannerly young man, he would also find himself in demand as an escort in the better social circles.

The business first at hand, however, was establishing the Pender troupe on new ground. It was a little frightening, despite the fact that the theater to which they were ordered to report had a comfortably familiar name, the Hippodrome. But what a contrast it was to the Bristol Hippodrome! Located on Sixth Avenue between 43rd and 44th Streets, its revolving stage stretched virtually the entire distance between the numbered thoroughfares. It had a ballet corps of eighty, a chorus of one hundred and required backstage employees numbering around eight hundred to mount a show that might have a cast of a thousand performers – drawn from all over the world. It could, and often did, present water ballets on its stage and it required its performers to check in for work at a time clock – not so much because the management was mean-spirited, but because this was the only way to keep track of everyone. The auditorium seated ten thousand people, making it the largest theater in the world.

The little Pender troupe, with its unpretentious if expert knockabout routines, was afraid it would be lost in these overwhelming precincts, but they were not, and they settled in for a run that lasted the season, and then were booked on the Keith circuit, the leading vaudeville wheel, for a tour that took them to the major eastern cities and well into 1922, when, finally, they returned to New York and the top of their profession – they played the Palace. Along the way the boys met a former President, Woodrow Wilson, and on the beach at Atlantic City, Archie saw Jack Dempsey, out for a peaceful swim, swarmed by a mob of autograph seekers who seemed to appear out of nowhere.

The tour forms one of Cary Grant's fondest memories – everything was so new, everything was so interesting, and the familial ties he felt to the Penders and the rest of the boys were unabated. Yet he had, as well, a gift for independence – the best legacy of his former life – and a forceful if unfocused ambition. When the tour ended, he and a couple of the other boys decided to stay on in America. And the fair-minded Pender staked them with the cash equivalent of their homeward fares, without mentioning the inconvenience and expense of finding and training replacements.

For Archie Leach his first months on his own were a bit of a scuffle. An Australian who would later become well known as the costume designer, Orry-Kelly, hand-painted neckties which Archie hawked for him on the streets. A little later, recruited to escort the opera singer Lucrezia Bori to a dinner party (she sensed his poverty and kindly insisted on walking to and from it to spare him the cab fares) he met George Tilyew, the entrepreneur who owned Steeplechase Park, and got a job from him as a stilt-walker, advertising that Coney Island attraction by stalking up and down in front of it – and trying to avoid the little boys determined to trip him up. After that he joined forces with some other Pender refugees and some Americans, and they worked up an act for the Hippodrome, which they then toured on a circuit somewhat less grand than the Keith, working their way through Canada, and along the American west coast, where they played Los Angeles among other cities. The act broke up some time in 1924, and for a time Archie did a bit of this and a bit of that in vaudeville – he worked with jugglers and a unicycle rider, he was the audience plant in a mind-reading act, and he was a straight man for comedians. If there is anything that unifies this diversity it is that all his jobs required impeccable timing, a good-natured ability to keep your eyes open and your mind alert for the cues, and a talent for self-effacement. If, as one believes, he has the best comic timing of any leading man in film history, and if, as Kael suggests, he is also the least narcissistic of actors, those admirable qualities were polished in this period.

Vaudeville, of course, was a dead end; one broke out of it by way of revues like the *Ziegfeld Follies*, but as a rule only if one had a unique talent, a speciality. The likes of Will Rogers and W. C. Fields made it, but mainly because they combined their gift for comedy with their specialities, in the one case rope-twirling, the other juggling. Archie Leach's gifts were not of that sort. He was not a soloist. And, in any event, the medium was slowly dying. The movies (Archie often worked the stage bills that preceded feature films in many houses) and in the latter part of the 1920s, radio, were cutting into its audience as well as well as drawing away its headliners.

Some time in 1927, when he was back in New York, a friend suggested he make the switch to legit, and introduced him to Reggie Hammerstein, Oscar's younger brother and nephew of the producer Arthur Hammerstein, who gave him an audition. A few years before the thought would have terrified him; when he left the Pender troupe he had yet to speak a line on stage. Now he had got away with many that were doubtless anything but polished. He had presence, he had the confidence born of richly varied experience, he had a light, pleasant singing voice, and, as they would continue to do for years, his looks were improving with the passage of time, the sharp over-handsomeness of his youthful features mellowing with matur-

ity. He made the transition with apparent ease, though oddly no one thought to cast him in a farce or a romantic comedy, the sorts of shows that, in adaptation or imitation, would form the basis of the film genres with which he would be indelibly associated. Hammerstein did operettas, and that meant Archie Leach would, too. He opened at Hammerstein's new theater (which the producer named after himself) playing the second lead in *New Dawn*, a show for which Oscar Hammerstein provided the lyrics. The role was that of an Australian, which may have added to the confusion about his origins that beset his Broadway friends. It was short-lived, and Hammerstein replaced him out of town in the next show he did for the producer, after which Marilyn Miller asked for

As a Shubert leading man, left, and as promising side of Hollywood beefcake, *c.* 1932.

him as a replacement for her leading man in *Rosalie*, but Hammerstein and that show's producer, Florenz Ziegfeld, were enemies, and Archie's contract was sold to the Shuberts. He did something called *Boom Boom*, which starred Jeanette MacDonald, he did a version of *Die Fledermaus* that opened two days after the stock market crash and itself quickly crashed. After that came a successful summer season at the St Louis Municipal Opera and then return to New York, where the Shuberts loaned him out for *Nikki*, which starred Fay Wray and was written by her husband of the time, John Monk Saunders, a flyer in the First World War who seems to have written most of the movies constituting the aviation genre. Indeed, this show was based on one of his screenplays, *The Last Flight*, in which Richard Barthelmess had played the role Archie Leach did during the brief Broadway run.

When this show closed, he decided it was time to take what he called a vacation, but which was actually a scouting trip to Hollywood. He was not unhappy with what he had been doing. For several years now his salary had been between $300 and $450 a week. He had a Packard car, a convertible, which pleased him, plenty of amusing friends and a promising enough career ahead of him on the stage. On the other hand, the movies, now that they could talk, and sing, presented the most interesting possibilities.

Indeed, a little flirtation had begun between the man and the medium. At the time they were doing *Boom Boom*, both he and Jeanette MacDonald had been screen-tested by Paramount's east coast studio, but though she got the contract that led to her starring roles in the movie operettas Ernst Lubitsch so winningly directed for the studio, nothing came of it for Archie. The executives rather missed the point about him, it would seem, focusing their attention on on his thickish neck (which perhaps loomed larger in their eyes than it should have because he has the gymnast's narrow, sloping shoulders) and his slightly bow-legged walk, also not uncommon in men trained as he was. In 1931, however, around the time of *Nikki*, he returned to the same studio and did a one-reel short, *Singapore Sue*, in which as one of a group of American sailors in an oriental bar, he sings. If anything, he appears over-eager, over-energetic, again not an uncommon failing among stage performers doing their early films; actors as disparate as Olivier and Cagney had to overcome the same problem.

Given this ambiguous evidence regarding his screen potential, he was probably right to advertise his trip west modestly, as a vacation, and leave the door open for a return to the Shuberts, who said they would be glad to have him back.

33

# 3 THE GROUND UNDER HIS FEET

ONCE HE HAD BEGUN TO ESTABLISH HIMSELF ON Broadway there is a certain lack of dramatic tension in the upward progress of Archie Leach. As Pauline Kael says, the story of his career reads rather like that of a businessman heading for tycoonship, a politician making his way to the Presidency. He embraced, no doubt unconsciously, the basic conventions of their biographies, which segregate all hardship in the early years and show nothing of the ensuing struggles for advantage over rivals or with one's own demons. No doubt he had some of the latter – he has hinted at their existence from time to time – but in the old fashioned way of public men, he considered them no one's business but his own and avoided all discussion of them. The darkness of his childhood was deep and dangerous, might even be understood as a black hole forceful enough to have drawn a lesser fellow down and into obscurity, but since it did not, it could in retrospect be turned to account. It became, as the formative years did for so many men of his and earlier generations, an exemplary obstacle – *the* exemplary obstacle – that, surmounted and put behind, freed one from the need to discuss and psychoanalyse the subsequent ones.

Practically speaking, this experience of the hard-knock life gave to movie people of his and slightly older generations a toughness of spirit that subsequent generations – middle-class, educated in the colleges and the acting schools – lacked. Having known and survived worse than the moguls could hand out, they could, many of them, contemplate threats to their careers with equanimity, for they knew they could, if need be, do something else and get by as they had before. Better still, they conceived of themselves not as artists in the usual sense of the word, but as craftsmen practising a trade, and thus avoided debilitating struggles with their consciences about the artistic merit, or lack of same, in what they were doing.

In one of the most acute passages she ever wrote, Pauline Kael put the matter this way:

'He [Archie Leach] became a performer in an era in which learning to entertain the public was a trade; he worked at his trade, progressed, and rose to the top. He has probably never had the sort of doubts about acting which have plagued so many later performers, and he didn't agonise over choices, as actors of his stature do now. A young actor now generally feels that he is an artist only when he uses his technique for personal expression and for something he believes in. And so he has a problem that Archie Leach never faced: When actors became artists in the modern sense, they also became sellouts. They began to feel emasculated when they played formula roles that depended on technique only, and they had to fight themselves to retain their belief in the audience, which often preferred what they did when they sold out. They were up against all the temptations, corruptions, and conflicts that writers and composers and painters had long been wrestling with. Commerce is a bind for actors now in a way that it never was for Archie Leach; art for him was always a trade.'

Yes. Consider Archie Leach in Hollywood, standing on the brink of becoming Cary Grant. He was there quite logically. Between working in Shubert operettas and playing second leads and leads in program pictures, which was what he was about to do, what was there to choose? In the wayward way of show business both might lead to better things, but there was no way of predicting which offered the clearer path to full-scale stardom. Meantime, the Hollywood pay was as good, the weather infinitely better and the working conditions perhaps a shade more comfortable.

He had an introduction to Marion Gering a Paramount director, and it would seem that soon after his arrival he was also invited to have dinner with B. P. Schulberg, then head of production at Paramount's west coast studio. The director thought he could use Archie in a test he was doing with a young woman, and

Left, on the brink of becoming Cary Grant, he made close to one-tenth of his entire feature film output during his first year on the Paramount lot. Among those first seven titles was *Merrily We Go to Hell*, under Dorothy Arzner's direction. The stars were Sylvia Sidney and Fredric March. Grant appeared mainly in the play-within-the film sequences (below) as the star of newsman-playwright March's attempt to win Broadway fame and fortune.

'Amiable' and 'efficient' were words heard among the faint critical phrases applied to Grant in his first feature, *This is the Night*. Playing an Olympic javelin thrower, he received fifth billing, beneath character men like Charles Ruggles and Roland Young, who would soon enough be supporting him. Even Lily Damita, who would achieve her largest fame as Errol Flynn's 'tempestuous' mate a decade later, was billed above Grant, and appears to have him roughly where she wants him in the still below left. His fourth 1932 film, *The Devil and the Deep* placed him in somewhat grander company, with Charles Laughton and Tallulah Bankhead (above). He played the young officer who supplied the reason for Laughton to be insanely jealous of Bankhead, playing his wife.

Schulberg approved the plan. He had nothing to lose – and if the young man (Archie was now twenty-seven) looked good his success could be used as a weapon in the executive's perpetual war with his rivals back east, who having passed on his earlier test could be shown to have no eye for up and coming talent. The test was fine – from Archie Leach's point of view. He was offered a contract at $450 a week. The woman with whom he tested was offered nothing, and was not heard from again.

The only problem was that faintly risible name of his – Archie Leach. It might do for a comic, a best-friend type, but not for a leading man. It was proposed that he use the name of the character he had played in *Nikki* – Cary Lockwood. Cary was all right with the studio executives, but Lockwood was longish for the marquees and, anyway, there was another young actor around with the same patronymic. Someone hauled out a list of short Anglo–Saxon last names kept handy for this purpose, and his moving finger stopped at Grant. 'Cary Grant.' It sounded all right to Archie Leach. And so, quite casually, he put behind him the last visible remnant of his past.

He would later admit that 'cautiously' peering out from behind an assumed name, an assumed identity really, had both disadvantages as well as its advantages ('If I couldn't clearly see out, how could anyone see in?') but it would seem that the latter outweighed the former. He could see all that he needed to see, and he had small interest in letting strangers have anything like an intimate glimpse into his life.

Indeed, so well hidden was his life that there is even a certain confusion about the public record. Many people, for example, still believe that it was Mae West who discovered him, but that is not true. In his first year he made seven films at Paramount, none of them with West. Nor were all of them entirely obscure – only most of them. He began in second leads and even smaller parts, and it was not until his fifth film that he worked in something anyone on the lot cared very much about. This was *Blonde Venus*, fourth of the six pictures Marlene Dietrich did for the studio under the guidance of her discoverer and mentor, Josef Von Sternberg. It was undoubtedly the most feeble of the lot, lacking as it did those whimsies of decor and melodrama that give films like *Morocco, Shanghai Express* and *The Scarlet Empress* their enduring status as classics of conscious exoticism and unconscious comedy.

Grant appears as the second man in a triangle involving Dietrich and Herbert Marshall, her inventor-husband who falls ill as a result of his work with radium and requires a trip to Germany for a cure. To obtain the money for it, and to support their child, she goes to work as a nightclub singer, where Grant, a shady political boss ('he runs this end of town'), meets her and takes her as his mistress – which definitely helps out at home. In his first scene he decisively punches out another character, but the rest of the time he is still very much wrapped in the cocoon of his good looks, so self-effacing that he almost disappears. For his part to have worked at all, he should have been directed to play in vivid contrast to Marshall, who aside from his witty performance for Lubitsch in *Trouble in Paradise* (his next film), always played civility as if it were a form of victimisation. But Von Sternberg had Grant throw away even his passionate speeches; a declaration of obsessive love, for example, was delivered with no emphasis, and became, if anything, a declaration of indifference. The film, one imagines, was intended to modify Dietrich's image, to show that she could suffer for her sins the way so many other leading women of the moment were doing, and this she extensively did as the picture rambled along, looking for the dramatic tension it never found. It made only one lasting contribution to Grant's career. At some point before shooting began Von Sternberg reached out his stern *auteur*'s hand and brushed the actor's hair, changing its part-

In *Blonde Venus* Grant finally had a leading leading lady, Marlene Dietrich, and a leading director, Josef von Sternberg. But he was still cast in a secondary role, while the script was strictly tertiary in the least of the six collaborations between the great pictorialist director and the star he made. Some critics, however, were beginning to write that Grant deserved better things than he was getting.

ing from the left side to the right, where it has remained ever since – a distinct improvement.

In the short run, the picture was good for Grant's career. The executives took serious notice of him for the first time (as did critics and audiences when the picture went into release) and he was rewarded with his first lead (as a small town playboy with a smashing wardrobe in *Hot Saturday*, modestly hinting at things to come). Much more important was his casting as Lieutenant Pinkerton in *Madame Butterfly*, with a screenplay based on Belasco's old drama with Puccini's music from the opera based on the same source used only as thematic material in the underscoring. This film was a personal project of B. P. Schulberg, who had chosen the role of Cio-Cio San for his great and good friend of the time, Sylvia Sidney. Grant's casting opposite her was a sure sign that his first year at hard labor had not been in vain. The film, however, was judged heavy and turgid, and its failure was a factor in Schulberg's dismissal from his job a little later.

It was also a factor, however, in bringing Grant to Mae West's attention. She had come west trailing vague clouds of scandal (the police kept obligingly raiding the plays she devised for herself to parade her languid innuendoes) and she had been a success opposite George Raft in *Night after Night*, a dim little drama that had been a surprising hit. Now, on the verge of bankruptcy, Paramount decided to offer her the chance to adapt some of her stage material for the screen. Whatever the credits read, she was the *de facto* writer and director of *She Done Him Wrong*, which was an adaptation of her most famous stage piece, *Diamond Lil*. Also its casting director. She spotted Grant on the lot, thought he looked like her kind of hunk, and inquired after him. Told he was working on *Madame Butterfly*, she is alleged to have replied, 'If he can talk, I'll take him.'

He could, and she did, and although he has always been generous in crediting her for the instruction she gave in such matters as timing

Grant was likely-looking in riding habit and in black tie (or white). But he was unlikely, if not downright uncomfortable, as a crooked political boss, called upon to punch out a night club boor and to keep Dietrich. At an amusement park (below) he and his *Blonde Venus* were joined by Carole Lombard and Richard Barthelmess, both of whom would be co-stars in the future.

and take 'ems, the fact is that he was very passive in his scenes with her. His more recent remark that he and most of the other members of the cast and crew were afraid of West seems nearer to the mark He did not exactly back away from her, but he was quietly, even awkwardly content to do what men always did around West in her pictures, endure a radical role reversal. They, not the woman, are the sex objects in them, and her pursuit, however good natured and leisurely, was none the less implacable.

'You can be had,' she famously said to him, and his response is not a riposte, but a sort of well-bred embarrassment. It suited his role, that of an undercover police officer posing as a Bowery missionary in order to gain evidence that some of her associates are engaged in a white slavery ring. Indeed, if he had done nothing else in his career, he would have gained a tiny immortality as the recipient of the most famous, and most misquoted, line she ever uttered. It was not, "*C*'mon up and see me sometime,' but: 'Why don't you come up sometime and see me,' which after his near-inarticulate refusal she reiterates thus: 'Come on up. I'll tell your fortune.'

Actually, of course, she helped to make his fortune. For *She Done Him Wrong*, the only West picture that was produced with some care, mounted with some regard for professional standards, was a huge hit, often credited with saving the studio from going under. And association with a hit was useful to Grant just then. It would keep the studio interested in him and audiences on the look-out for him.

Later in this same year – 1933 – quickly cashing in on the success of *She Done Him Wrong*, the studio threw him together with West again in *I'm No Angel*. In this one he was a playboy-lawyer seeking to loosen her clutches on a friend whom Mae has lured away from his fiancé, but falling into them himself. The picture probably contains more of her immortal one-liners than the first one did, including,

43

'Beulah, peel me a grape,' and, to Grant, 'When I'm good, I'm very good, but when I'm bad I'm better.' And it outdid its predecessor at the box office, though it is a thoroughly awful picture, static, stupefying, and watchable today only as a historical curiosity.

That line of West's – 'You can be had' – is regarded by Kael as emblematic of Grant's screen career, screen self:

'That was what the women stars of his greatest hits were saying to him for thirty years, as he backed away – but not too far. One after another, the great ladies courted him ... willing but not forward, Cary Grant must be the most publicly seduced male the world has known ... The little bit of shyness and reserve is pure box-office gold, and being the pursued doesn't make him seem weak or passively soft. It makes him glamorous – and since he is not as available as other men, far more desirable.'

And so on, for many pages.

Despite the many virtues of Pauline Kael's essay – and there is no critic whose eye for the telling detail in a performance is as sharp as hers – she is wrong in her implication that West was on to his essence in these films and wrong, as we will see later, to identify that essence as 'shyness and reserve'. It was part of his appeal, but only a part: his case is altogether more complicated than that. Which is not to say that he was not, with West and in nearly everything else he did in this period, almost dangerously recessive. He was – but one feels that it is not necessarily women and sex that make him that way. It is his whole situation at the time. One thinks of him in his Paramount pictures, which ranged through virtually every genre known to man in those days, as the new kid in school, the new boy on the block. He seems, for the most part, watchful, wary, hoping his good manners and appealing looks will carry him through the awkwardness of this new beginning. He does not put himself aggressively forward; he has the hopeful air about him of

someone waiting to be invited to join the play, become part of the gang. And he shows nothing of that wild, try-anything farcicality that is so much a part of the Cary Grant that would shortly emerge as the most obvious aspect of his screen personality, and the thing that would most obviously differentiate him from the other light romantic leads of the time.

The steady exposure he was getting was no bad thing. In a time when a major studio like Paramount was turning out the equivalent of a complete change of bills for its movie theater chains every week (a main feature, a supporting feature, short subjects, newsreel, what-have-you) it was important for a young star to gain exposure, no matter how. The public had to get used to you, comfortable with you, before it would start consciously looking for you, asking for you. So for a time it was all right for the studio executives to keep putting Grant in all kinds of different ventures. A sampling of the titles he was in, from the time of his first Mae West picture to the picture that, in 1936, finally enabled him to assert himself, tells the tale: *Alice in Wonderland, Thirty-Day Princess, Born to be Bad, Kiss and Make Up, Ladies Should Listen, Enter Madame, Wings in the Dark, The Last Outpost.* An all-star production of a 'classic', comedy romances, non-comedy romances, adventure romances, an aviation picture – one gets the sense that nobody at the studio quite understood what they had.

That, certainly, was Grant's impression. If anything, they seemed to want to use him as a second-string Gary Cooper, which is an idea that perhaps seems stranger in retrospect than it did at the time. The executives may have seen in Grant's diffidence before the cameras an analogy with the appearance of shyness that Cooper projected. They may well have seen in Grant's lack of visible ties, to any particular place, (through looks, accent or mannerisms), a quality usefully comparable to Cooper's ability to fit in almost anywhere. It is true that Cooper was born in the American west and

44

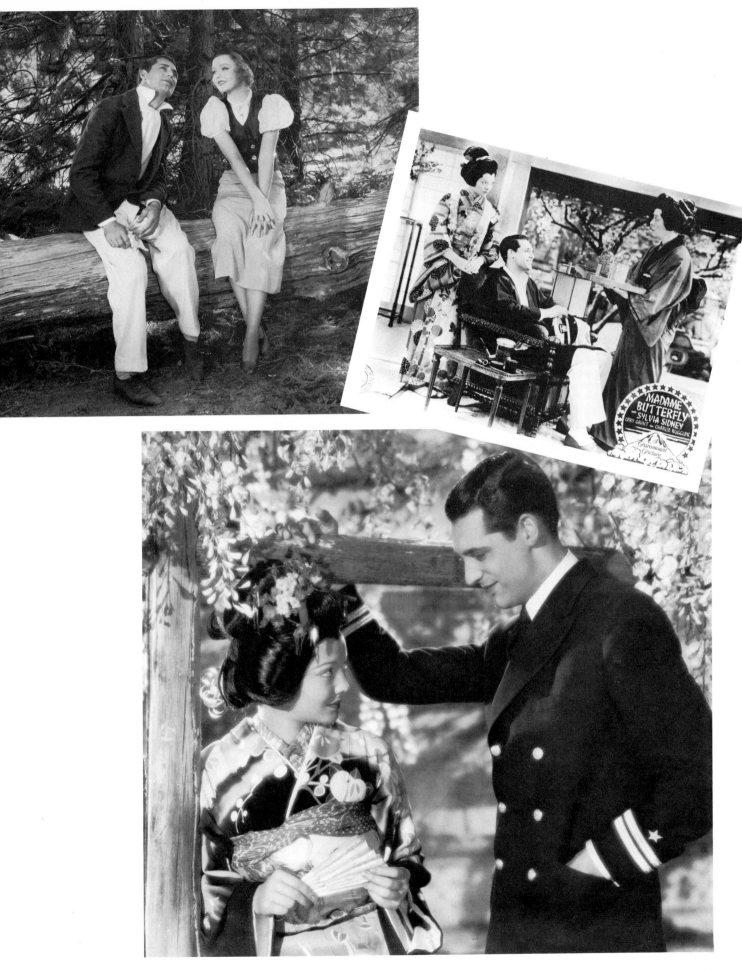

'You can be had.' Well, not really. But it is a thought that occurred to many a member of her sex after Mae West first proposed it in *She Done Him Wrong* in 1933. Grant played an undercover police officer in the film, and sensibly kept his talent for comedy undercover most of the time, too. He knew – and she knew – that the picture belonged to West. Later on, in 1955, they renewed acquaintance as equals.

**History does not record just what the Mae West prize was. But the film certainly wasn't. Still,** *I'm No Angel* **was, if anything, a bigger box office success than West's first collaboration with Grant. In this one he was a society lawyer smitten by her debatable charms.**

played in westerns from the beginning of his career to the end. But it also must be recalled that by this time he had already done *Morocco* with Dietrich for Von Sternberg, Hemingway's *A Farewell to Arms* and even Lubitsch's watery adaptation of Noël Coward's *Design for Living*, in which he had quite easily held up his share of the *ménage a trois* he shared with Fredric March and Miriam Hopkins. He had *The Lives of a Bengal Lancer* in his immediate future and, further ahead, a Marco Polo, a Beau Geste, another Lubitsch film and much other work in which he could wear his superbly tailored English suits to excellent advantage.

In those days the studios liked to keep what they thought of as copies of their star originals on hand to fill in if the more important players flatly turned down a role, and also as a veiled threat to them, a reminder that, as the moguls liked to say, anyone was replaceable. This was scarcely a position Grant relished, either as a performer or as a human being. And, as the years went by, he became increasingly aware of missed opportunities. One must wonder, certainly, why, when he was on the same lot with Lubitsch, someone did not think to put them together: Grant really was the actor the director was looking for and never quite found. And Paramount's refusal to lend him to MGM, which wanted him for the role Franchot Tone got in *Mutiny on the Bounty*, angered him and, it would seem, first turned his thoughts to leaving the studio and, perhaps, avoiding any similarly exclusive commitments in the future.

The question is, if the studio didn't know what Grant was, or might be, did Grant? Only partly, it would seem. After fifteen or twenty pictures (he would cram – be forced to cram – better than a quarter of a thirty-four-year career's output into his first four years) he may not have learned what or who he was, but he was beginning to have a glimmer of what he would like to become. And he was beginning

A trio to conjure with. Nöel Coward visits West and Grant on the Paramount lot (left). Below, a motley crowd gathers around the stars of *I'm No Angel* outside their sound stage.

to see that most of what he had been doing since he came to Hollywood was not that, and was not leading toward that.

Sensible craftsman that he was, with his strong sense of his own limits, and his medium's limit, no thought was spared for Hamlet. He was a hard and painstaking worker, but it is not written that gloom or anguish is its necessary concomitant. Laurence Olivier has recently codified, in his autobiography, the thought that must have occurred to Grant in those days: 'Except for playing light comedy to an enraptured audience, acting is not an enjoyable craft.' He would have enjoyment from his work. And he would give it, because the return on that was something he also required. 'Each of us is dying for affection...' he was to say almost a half-century later. 'Everything we do is affected by this longing. That's why I became an actor. I was longing for affection. I wanted people to like me.'

They did. Or they were beginning to. But only in a mild, tolerating sort of way. He needed more than that. And he was beginning to sense how that might be managed. He would have to take his hand out of his pocket.

This is the way he would later put it: 'The tough thing, the final thing, is to be yourself. That takes doing, and I should know. I used to be Noël Coward. Hand-plunged-in-the-pocket, y'know. It took me three long years to get my silly hand out of there, and they were three years wasted...' Four, actually – if you count from the release of his first feature to the release of the film that was to be the beginning of his deliverance. And, it cannot be emphasised strongly enough, it was only a beginning. For the role of Jimmy Monkley in *Sylvia Scarlett* was salutary for him not so much because of what it prefigured, but because of the opportunity it offered to get in touch with what was usable in his past, lay it out in public, and dis-

*Woman Accused* **cast Grant opposite Nancy Carroll again, this time in a shipboard romance** *cum* **murder mystery. It was more notable for its origins – as a magazine serial each chapter of which had been written by a popular hack of the moment – than for the end result. Among the writers whose work Grant and Co. tried to bring to life were Rupert Hughes, Vicki Baum, Zane Grey, Vina Delmar and Irvin S. Cobb. Just whose idea it was to get the hero into gaucho get-up is unknown.** *The Eagle and the Hawk* **was an altogether different matter. An anti-war aviation drama, based on a story by Grant's old friend, John Monk Saunders, and co-starring Fredric March, it is probably the best film Grant made at Paramount.**

cover that his bright new, light new world would not collapse inward upon him, that, indeed, it was capable of vast expansion.

It was a loan-out – to RKO – and why Paramount would go for so marginal an enterprise when it had refused to let him do something so expensively in the mainstream and self-consciously important as *Mutiny on the Bounty*, which would have enhanced his value to his home studio, is one of those mysteries of the executive mind best left unplumbed. For *Sylvia Scarlett*, based on a novel by Compton Mackenzie at his most fey would turn out to be neither a commercial nor a critical success. Its persistence as something of a cult film would later amuse its director, George Cukor and its star, Katharine Hepburn greatly, for the night of its preview was one of the worst in their careers, audience response being so dreadful that they offered to make another picture for their producer, Pandro Berman, free, as compensation. An offer he rejected, crying quite seriously, 'I don't want either of you ever to work for me again.'

One can see why it so befuddled everyone at the time. What a strange – not to say queer – little movie it is! There literally never has been, and never would be, any movie quite like it. Not quite a romance, not quite a comedy, it might best be described as a sort of brushed-off

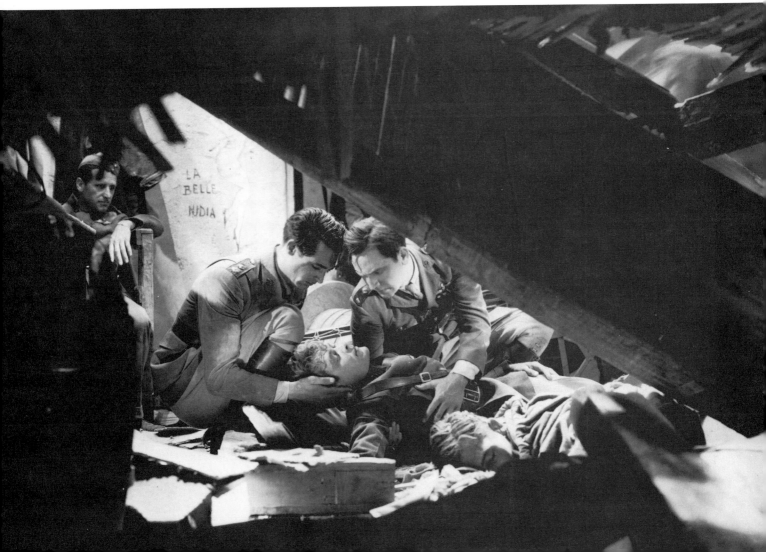

Ladies' Man. Among Grant's leading women, circa 1934–35 were Loretta Young in *Born to be Bad* (top left), Frances Drake in *Ladies Should Listen* (top right) Geneviève Tobin in *Kiss and Make Up* and Elissa Landi in *Enter Madame* (opposite). They don't make fireplaces like that anymore – not even in the movies.

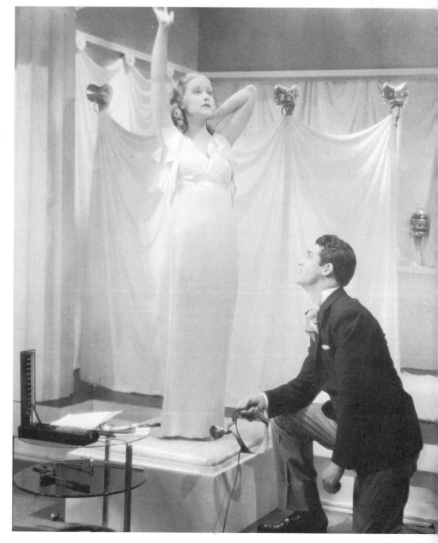

tragedy, in which nothing and no one is quite what they seem to be at first, and the characters' responses to the events of the story are often inappropriate, sometimes dislocatingly so. The oddities begin with Katharine Hepburn's title role, in which she appears for well over half the movie as a young man, a disguise she adopts to help her father – a bumbling embezzler played by Edmund Gwenn – escape from France before he is arrested for his crimes. They meet Jimmy Monkley on a boat crossing the English Channel, and having got the old man into trouble with Customs over some lace he is smuggling (in order to distract attention from his own activities in that line), Jimmy then casually inveigles the Scarletts into becoming his accomplices on some swindles in London, which, though quite cruel, the movie plays almost as comic pranks. Needing to lie low for a while, they take up the life of strolling players, working the more picturesque coastal towns, where the Gwenn character's love for an old girlfriend of Jimmy's who has joined them drives him first to madness, then to suicide. Hepburn, having had one woman make

High Adventures. In *Wings in the Dark* **Grant** played a blinded flyer who rescues a famous aviatrix (Myrna Loy) when a fog temporarily renders her sightless. Amelia Earhart (left) visited him on the set. *The Last Outpost* (opposite) once again put him in the role of the other man – this time coming between Claude Rains and Gertrude Michael. Both films were made in 1935.

A little bit of England comes to Laurel Canyon. And the bluffs beyond Malabu doubled for Dover's White Cliffs. But the principal oddity of *Sylvia Scarlett* was Katharine Hepburn disguising herself as a boy. And fetching she was opposite a Grant who also appeared as he never had before, playing a cockney con man with a wide streak of misanthropy in him.

overtures to her while dressed as a boy, now excites the interest of a male artist (Brian Aherne) while she is still in drag. The largest question of the movie then becomes whether he will still care for her when her true sexual identity is revealed. (The answer is 'yes', but perhaps not quite so rapturously.)

The picture, as the synopsis indicates, undergoes the most wilful mood changes, brightening and darkening unpredictably, and its failure when it was released doubtless has something to do with these oscillations as well as with its overturning of what the audience expected based on its understanding of generic conventions. It is, perhaps, no more stylised than most movies of its time, but its stylisation was entirely unlike anything anyone was familiar with; from its never-never vision of rural England, to its becharmed view of low-level theatrical life (the little company works in Pierrot–Pierrette costumes) to its presentation of the creative life (Aherne's artist is almost laughably smart-set, his studio home – a converted barn with a swing in its always open front door – so perfect in its decor that any real artist would be afraid to get a splash of paint on the floor).

Yet it seemed to liberate Grant. He had never worked with a director of Cukor's quality, a man with a gift for creating a climate in which an actor or an actress could find things in themselves that they didn't know they had. Nor had he ever had a leading woman of Hepburn's spirit, either. And however loopy the story they were engaged in trying to tell, the contrast between it and the utterly routine things he had been doing at Paramount was not lost on him. George Cukor remembered: 'He was a successful young leading man who was nice looking but had no particular identity. In fact, if you see him with Mae West, he's rather awkward. But ... in *Sylvia Scarlett* he flowered; he felt the ground under his feet.'

That ground was native ground, and one is speaking in more than the geographical sense. One imagines that the almost manic-depressive

mood swings of the picture matched his sense, which experience had taught him, of how suddenly, shockingly the taste and tone of life could change. More important, Jimmy, the Cockney swindler, was formed, at least in part, by the forces, the society, that had shaped Grant. First glimpsed in a black coat and hat, a watcher in the shadows on that Channel boat, he later describes himself satirically as a 'little friend to all the world, nobody's enemy but me own', more soberly as 'a rolling stone, an adventurer', who is neither a 'sparrow' nor an ''awk' – the two principal categories into which the world's population falls, as he cynically sees it.

The analogy is obvious: both Jimmy and Grant have pasts they do not wish to discuss in any great detail, a sense that all alliances are shifting and temporary (Grant's first marriage, to Virginia Cherrill – the blind girl beloved by Chaplin in *City Lights* – contracted in 1933 was breaking up around this time). Above all, both actor and character share a sense that a man is mainly responsible for his own survival – no small difficulty – and only after that for the

formation of any fate he can manage that is of grander proportions, since no one is going to help much, or for long, with either problem. We don't know, of course, precisely what Jimmy's background was – probably even less elevated than Grant's – but the actor had no trouble in understanding its dreariness and the kind of radical self-reliance it required to climb up out of it, the alienation and the incapacity to sustain love or intimacy for very long when those qualities are invisible in a cold, or merely economically hard-pressed, family.

The major difference between Grant and his Jimmy, and the thing which gives the latter a near-tragic air, lies in their class sense. In both it is extraordinarily acute. If Grant went into theater because it was a classless world, one in which he could live outside the constraints of the social structure as the rest of us endure them, Jimmy has chosen to live on the criminal margin for the same reason. The difference between them, of course, is that Grant had the intelligence to act shrewdly on this assessment of things, using the glamour of his profession for entrée, to work his way through the inter-

*Scarlett* **days – and nights. Edmund Gwenn played Sylvia's weakling Dad. Dennie Moore (above right) was Maudie Tilt, the woman who drove Gwenn to despair and suicide in this curious blend of comedy, tragedy and romance.**

stices of the class barriers in order to better himself. For Jimmy, however, those barriers are solid, he can see no breaks in them, only the possibility of breaking himself against them. 'I'll give you a word of advice,' he warns Sylvia, 'don't try to step out of your class.' And he himself dares not aspire even to Sylvia, only a small step above him on the social scale. The best he can do, when the possibility is presented to him is to propose that they 'muck along' together for a while. But even that is not possible. He is too self-destructively cynical even for a fairly realistic romantic like Sylvia. 'You have the mind of a pig,' she says to him towards the end of the movie, when he shows himself entirely unmoved by her father's death. 'It's a pig's world,' he says, either knowingly or unknowlingly speaking the epitaph for his best hopes – and, incidentally, ours, since he is so much more devilishly attractive than the bland Aherne.

Jimmy Monkley was, in effect, Cary Grant's dark side – a cautionary figure. In him there is something of what Elias Leach had been, something of what Archie Leach might have been had he not been blessed with looks and energy and the wit to imagine for himself a better self, living in a better place. It is no wonder that suddenly in this role he forgot his manners, abandoned his passivity – and attacked. Attacked as he never had before. 'Cary Grant's romantic elegance is wrapped around the resilient, tough core of a mutt,' Kael says, 'and Americans dream of thoroughbreds while identifying with mutts. So do moviegoers the world over.' But there is even more to it than that. Some mutts touch us with their guts and their independence. But some scare us with their total unpredictability, their dangerous possibilities, as Jimmy Monkley did.

Now that he saw their possibilities, and his ability to control them – no matter how dashing he was, no matter how romantic he was – a little bit (and sometimes a lot) of those qualities would show in almost everything Cary Grant did for the next few years. It is what, finally, made Cary Grant Cary Grant – and not Melvyn Douglas.

# BRINGING UP CARY

IF 'SYLVIA SCARLETT' LIBERATED CARY GRANT AS an actor, if it suggested the possibilities inherent in taking some time off *from* good behavior, it represented only a beginning for him. He had yet to begin the process of self-creation (actually self-re-creation) by which he would make his permanent mark in the world. Even so, it is interesting how quickly he would proceed now that he could see what could be done with himself if he set his mind to it. This is especially so when one remembers how deeply Grant himself believed that he had a rather larger identity problem than most people had. He did not, he thought have the slightest clue as to who he was. Or, if he did, he was not entirely certain that he liked what he was, or that other people would either. He was, possibly, being over-sensitive on the point. But this being the case it seems that he decided, quite consciously, to make up a character that he liked and felt easy with. He has been, over the years, quite insistent on this point. While he was still active as an actor he told an interviewer, 'I pretended to be a certain kind of man on screen, and I became that man in life. I became me.' As recently as 1981, looking back on things, he expanded on that thought to another reporter, 'I don't know that I've any style at all. I just patterned myself on a combination of Jack Buchanan, Noël Coward and Rex Harrison. I pretended to be somebody I wanted to be and I finally became that person. Or he became me. Or we met at some point. It's a relationship.'

Doubtless it is a more complicated relationship than he made it seem – since it was in the character he finally invented for himself to try to make things look easy and slightly comical. There is obviously more to the public Cary Grant than a combination of the people he named, and more to that creature that is drawn out of his personal history than he cares to admit. Then, too, contributions came in from the outside – from directors who sensed in him certain qualities useful to them and brought them out, from bits and pieces of the scripts he did, from the overall conventions of the genres in which he most frequently worked – that clung to him. One cannot help but feel, however, that part of the greatness of the great period of his career – the five years that began in 1937 when he did *Topper* and ended with *Suspicion* in 1941, that period in which he placed his unlooseable grip on our imaginations and our affections – stems in part from his own excitement about what he was discovering in himself, his own pleasure in trying things out, trying things on, a pleasure that seems to have had an infectious effect on everyone around him.

Not the least of the elements in his good mood was confidence. *Sylvia Scarlett* may have been a disaster for the studio, and no help at all to the other people involved with him in it, but for Grant it was breakthrough. He was singled out in the reviews and he was finally singled out in the executive screening rooms around Hollywood as something more than a pretty face. It was his ticket to leave Paramount where his contract was about to run out. His success in the film, combined with stuff the studio threw at him when he returned (a mystery called *Big Brown Eyes*, a loan-out to MGM for a second-lead in *Suzy*, a fizzled screwball comedy called *Wedding Present*) made up his mind for him finally. Not only would he not renew with Paramount, he would commit himself exclusively to no one. If his job was literally to find himself then he was going to do it on his own; he was not going to accept other people's judgments about what was right for him and his career.

At the time it was an astonishing and courageous decision. Stars who were far better established than he was cleaved to their studios, could not imagine themselves acting as independants. No one of his stature had attempted to conduct a freelance star career since the 1920s and those who tried it now were people whose contracts had been dropped by their

*Big Brown Eyes* (this page) cast Grant as a detective, Joan Bennett as a manicurist, joining forces to bring jewel thief-killers to justice. Raoul Walsh directed this half-screwball in his customary headlong manner. *Suzy*, with Franchot Tone and Jean Harlow (opposite, above) had Grant up in the air again as an aviator lured astray (and finally to his death by Benita Hume (Mrs Ronald Colman). *Wedding Present* re-teamed Bennett and Grant less successfully.

incomprehensible series of mergers and acquisitions, lurching along the edge of financial disaster most of the time, with a variety of management grabbing at this and that hope of temporary salvation. But like Columbia, it was a place where a number of independent, talented spirits would find refuge over the years. By signing non-exclusive arrangements with both of them Grant assured himself the right to pick and choose the best projects each had to offer, to participate in the shaping of those enterprises – and to go elsewhere if something interesting turned up.

It was, in fact, elsewhere that produced his next significant picture, for, curiously, he floundered at first in freedom almost as badly as he had in servitude to Paramount. There was

studios and were now scuffling along ignominiously in what was sometimes called 'one-shot city'. But he had come a long way on his own, a longer way than most, and it was clear to him that even if his sense of himself was still somewhat unformed, it was none the less better formed than that of the strangers behind the big desks at Paramount. And there were two studios then occupying somewhat ambiguous positions in the Hollywood pecking order that had need of someone like Grant. One of them was Columbia, struggling up from poverty row largely on the strength of Frank Capra's then-infallible comic touch. Harry Cohn, the legendary monster who ran the place almost single-handed, had learned from his experience with Capra that comedies were relatively inexpensive to make and, by and large, turned splendid profits. He had on hand, therefore, a number of writers and directors who were good at that sort of thing, and Grant would clearly be right for ideas as yet unborn by the likes of Leo McCarey, Robert Riskin and Sidney Buchman. At RKO the story was the opposite; it was the only studio with a significant life in American film history that never had a figure like Cohn to shape its personality. It was a pure corporate construction, the result of an almost

a feeble comedy made in England for Grand National, a Grace Moore musical at Columbia, and a curiosity, *The Toast of New York*, at RKO. It was a highly fictionalised, comic account of the rise of robber baron Jim Fisk. He was played by Edward Arnold, in an obvious attempt to repeat the success of a previous characterisation along these lines, in Howard Hawks' excellently ambiguous *Come and Get It*. Arnold's co-star from that venture, the self-destructive and gifted Frances Farmer, was in this film, too, and Grant, who was supposed to provide her love interest, was rendered, by her own account, quite stand-offish by her neurotic working habits.

The elsewhere film – the film that started him moving firmly in the right direction – was made about as far elsewhere as you could get and still remain respectable in American movies – at Hal Roach's little comedy studio, specialising in Laurel and Hardy pictures in Culver City, but now attempting to make one large budget picture annually. This year, the choice was *Topper*, in which Grant and Constance Bennett (who looked and acted very like Carole Lombard in the role) appeared as George and Marion Kerby, 'beautiful people' long before the term was invented, wastrels by the standards of the film's title character, Cosmo Topper (Roland Young, more often seen in more acerbic and eccentric roles, but every bit as effective as the Milquetoast he was here). He is president of the bank in which the Kerbys are principal stockholders, appalled but just slightly envious of their flighty ways, especially since he is near-terminally henpecked at home (by Billie Burke). When the Kerbys carelessly kill themselves by wrapping their smart car around a tree, they are required to do a good deed before they can ascend to heaven. This, they decide, should take the form of freeing Topper from the tyranny of respectability. Materialising and dematerialising at will, they sow delightful havoc in every corner of Cosmo's life, but finally get the poor man loosened up suffi-

ciently to say so. As his feet do a little dance step, as if guided by a will of their own, while the rest of his body remains stock still, he cries, rather poignantly, 'I can learn to live after all.'

The picture has none of the richness or comic resonance of the truly great comedies of the era – it is pure gimmickry. But it was commercially successful, and for Grant it was an important picture on two counts. He had, of course, been shown to look superb in black tie (or white) in more than one role before this, but now for the first time the attitudes that we like to see men put on when they don formal wear were fully demonstrated – ease and charm, of course, but something more as well: a capacity for what might be called comfortable dominance. There was nothing pushy about it (although there was obviously a lot of sheer mischief in his prankishness, if not downright devilry), but for the first time he was in command of a situation, in charge of the picture, really, and lightly and gracefully so.

For purposes of the plot he was in this respect a literally magical figure. And some of that magical quality adhered to him. It would not be the last time he would play an otherworldly figure, but even when he did not he would henceforth (except in the very wildest farces) seem to us endowed with almost supernatural powers of knowingness, of what to say, what to wear, what to do in almost any social or sexual situation. Many of the stories in which he would later involve himself would, of course, have at their center an absolutely devastating attack on his impeccability and his aplomb, but these were never his fault, and the cream of the jest lay in his exasperated efforts to keep those qualities intact even if, for some reason, he had lost his pants, let's say, or unaccountably found himself meeting strangers while covered in a woman's negligée. In the latter part of his career, unfortunately, the magical element in his screen character would become over-developed, become almost a coat of invisible armor – and, given the wrong

script or careless direction, it could lead to a certain smugness. But that was many years in the future. At this juncture in his career, *Topper* functioned almost like a superb studio still. Contemplating it, one takes in what was to become, in the popular mind anyway, the pure essence of his image – playful and unflappable sophistication. There was, after its release, a huge jump in his fan mail – to some two hundred letters a week.

*Topper* had another function that was scarcely less important. It provided the moment at which Grant definitely linked himself to what has come to seem in retrospect the most memorable, the shortest-lived and the least carefully defined film genre of the era, the screwball comedy. By common consent, the picture that began the cycle was Frank Capra's *It Happened One Night* in 1934. (With assists from *The Thin Man* and *Twentieth Century* made in the same year). And indeed, Capra's film contained many of the basic elements that would become so deliciously familiar in the years immediately ahead – a headstrong heiress; a male lead (and a newspaperman at that, as so many of them were in films of this kind) representing the reality principle bedevilled; a rich *pater familias* who, being self made, is more democratic than most of the snobs and fools he is forced to associate with because of his new status; a romantic confusion requiring heroically loony exertions to sort it out. The picture, like most of Capra's work, nowadays strikes one as more sweetly romantic, far less gloriously wacked out, than its successors – so much so that one almost feels like dissenting from all that consenting. But surely it did represent a distinct and original shift in the comic tone of movies, and because it was a large popular and critical success, it did inspire imitations. And imitations of the imitations, until a set of self-perpetuating comic conventions were established and the genre took on not only a life of its own, but a dizzying, infectious quality as well. There were not that many purely

screwball comedies (offhand one thinks only of *My Man Godfrey, Bringing Up Baby* and *His Girl Friday*) but as Richard Corliss has suggested, the genre 'occupied a halfway house between knockabout farce and the more genteel brands of romantic comedy', which means that its free spirit could reach out and liberate just about any film produced in Hollywood that was intended to be funny. There is scarcely an American comedy after 1935 (and before 1940) that did not have elements of the screwball spirit in it. There were, in that time, very few farces about poor people (screwballism was purely a disease of the wealthy) and very few romantic comedies in which the well-dressed did not finally fall into the swimming pool or get zanily stranded in some improbable and embarrassing situation, often involving the loss of correct wardrobe.

Pauline Kael has argued, in her famous 'Raising Kane' essay, which sought to restore proper credit to comedy writer Herman Mankiewicz for his contribution to *Citizen Kane*, that the source of this spirit so linked in our minds with Hollywood in the 1930s was actually the Broadway of the 1920s. She is very persuasive on the point, for it is certainly true that when sound had eventually come to the movies, a Hollywood desperate for people who could write dialogue had drawn on a large group of New York writers to fill its needs. Some of them had journalism of the most cynical sort in their backgrounds, and most of that crowd had moved on to the bright young magazines of the bright young things of the 1920s. (*The American Mercury, The Smart Set, Vanity Fair, The New Yorker*), and from there to not entirely successful excursions into playwrighting where they competed with another group who had skipped journalism to concentrate on the theater from the start.

In New York at that time there was considerably freer passage between journalism, Broadway and literature than there is now, and in the speakeasies where everyone foregathered

**Elegant apparitions. Grant and Constance Bennett as the ghostly, cheerful George and Marion Kerby in** *Topper* **(1937).**

there was plenty of opportunity to observe the loopy rich taking their leisure as well. In this milieu one sees the social mix that would be placed on the stage at the time, and in the movies later. The less-well-known *litterateurs* admired the hard-hearted gag-writing of people like George S. Kaufman and Morrie Ryskind (who were important contributors, it should be noted, to developing the style of the Marx Brothers, whose films, in due course, contributed something to the manic spirit of screwballism).

People at Kaufman's level could drop in on Hollywood when the price was right without loss of critical regard or social status. They could also afford to come home and write satires of it like *Once in a Lifetime*, which, sweet irony here, they could then sell to the movies. But the younger and/or less successful members of the speakeasy crowd did not enjoy these options. They were forced to go west and stay there, which was a fate, for them, not as bad as F. Scott Fitzgerald and his biographers

have made it sound. They found that they fitted in on the coast more easily than could writers with grander conceptions of themselves and their gifts. They were fully as capable as their betters of satirising the town's pretences and insecurities, its materialism and its childishness, which they sometimes even got to do on screen, but were always free to do around their swimming pools. More to the point, they had worked to order in many a less profitable situation, did not mind writing collaboratively and had no snobbery about doing adaptations – especially when these turned out to be screen versions of the kinds of plays and novels and stories they had admired and imitated when they were hanging around Broadway.

As we have seen, Cary Grant knew some of these people when he was a young actor in New York, but what is astonishing is how many of their names pass through his filmography from 1936 onward: Robert Riskin, Dudley Nichols, Donald Ogden Stewart, Joel Sayre, Sam and Bella Spewack, Charles Lederer, Morrie Ryskind, Sidney Buchman, Ben Hecht, Norman Krasna, Joseph Mankiewicz (Herman's brother). Not all the films they wrote for him were screwball or even demi-screwball – some of them were comedies only by a long stretch of the imagination. But we are talking about a mood, a tone here, and this was the great collective contribution of these men and the kindred spirits they encountered in Hollywood (Jules Furthman, for example, who had been writing there since 1915, and Billy Wilder, who immigrated from Germany in 1933). Linked with directors like Howard Hawks, Cukor, Leo McCarey and George Stevens, they unintentionally created a screen form that was uniquely American and something that caused two excellent critics, considering what they wrought, to reach far afield from the movies to try to catch its essence. Stanley Kauffman, for instance, put it this way: 'Every scene is played faster than necessary, including love scenes, as if the speed knob on the phono-

Their revels now are ended. After a night on the town, the Kerbys draw a crowd as they wait snoozily for their bank to open. Driving their absolutely glorious automobile rather too speedily into a tree turns them into ectoplasmic presences a little later in *Topper*.

graph had been turned ahead slightly, and all the dialogues written in tight-packed wise-cracks which *sounds* like life, but really is the 20th century American theater's equivalent of blank verse ... an American convention, an abstraction.' Blank verse! Yes, that's good. But earlier Otis Ferguson, one of Kauffman's predecessors in the critic's chair at *The New Republic*, said 'these pictures' had 'a styling, a speed, and lightness and frequency of absurd surprise that combined sight, sound motion and recognition into something like music.' Something like music! That's good, too.

Not that there were many critics of Ferguson's discernment writing at the time. The praise of most reviewers, when it was granted, was chuckly-dismissive, and, of course, the armies of the left saw Hollywood's compulsive attraction to zany comedy as yet more evidence – as if any were needed – of its failure to recognise the needs of the audience for political education, for a realistic reflection of social and economic conditions in a depression, of geo-political events that increasingly suggested the inevitability of war. The audience, naturally got all the information it needed about the former down at the shop, and all the news of the latter that it required from the radio and newspapers. What it liked at the movies was to see rich, pretty, nice but rather silly people falling about, getting into jams that ordinary, commonsensical people (who often appeared in these pictures scratching their heads, looking bemused and sometimes being instrumental in setting things to rights) would never think of getting into. It was refreshing, it was pleasing, it was funny, and the art we now impute to these films was never self-conscious or even particularly visible and therefore off-putting to people in search of a little escape. Moreover, the sense these pictures conveyed of a world disrupted and not being put together again exactly as it had been, suited people's sense of how things were now going in the world generally. Maybe these pictures had more political

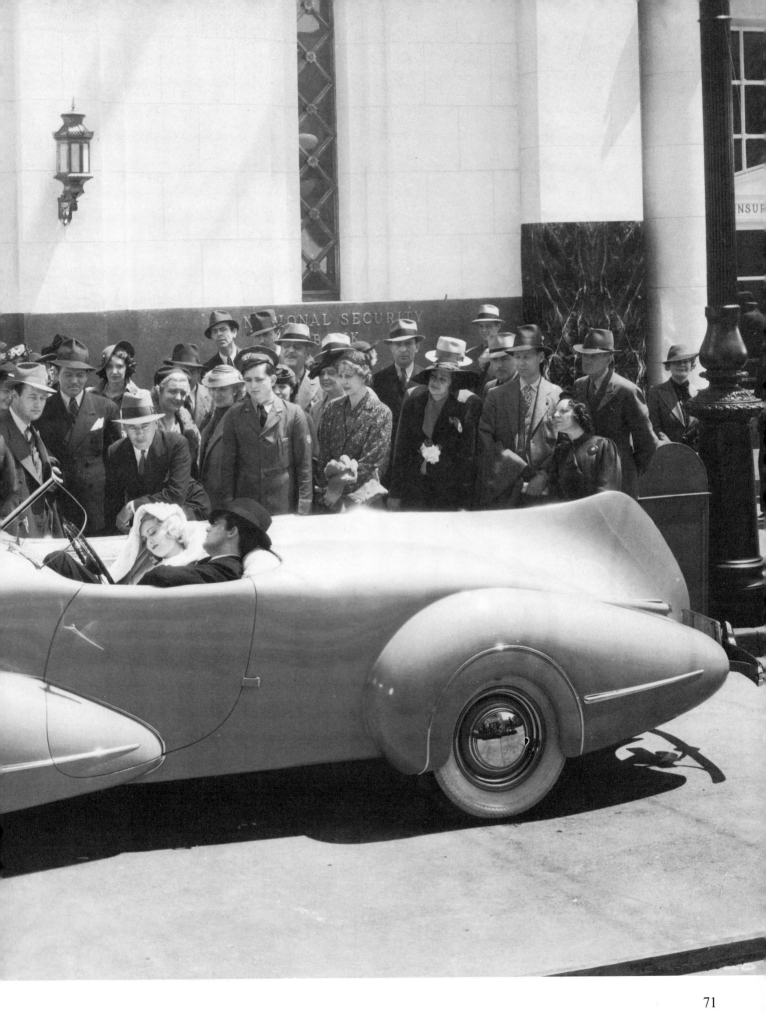

acuity than they were credited with at the time. But no matter – and no wonder these comedies were about as surefire in their profitability as anything the studios turned out in these years.

With *Topper*, then, Cary Grant was joining what amounts to the mainstream of American film-making at this historical moment. And he was joining it as it was about to crest. Yes, he had been in one or two modest efforts along this line at Paramount, but they had not been top-of-the-line stuff. And, yes, *Topper* itself was not top-of-the-line either, though taken together with the previous year's *The Ghost Goes West* it would direct the attention of the comic muse towards the risible possibilities of the supernatural. Be that as it may, everyone was now ready. The writers had the basic form down pat; the directors, many of whom had begun their careers in silent comedy, had their moves smoothly practised. And Grant had found himself. If *Sylvia Scarlett* had permitted him to explore the darker side of his gift without rendering him charmless, then *Topper* had given him the opportunity of projecting pure charm and seeing that even in an incorporeal state, he did not achieve complete weightlessness, an evanescence that would have rendered him inconsequential in the eyes of the public. For the next few years he would work on the middle ground defined by these two poles, establishing a character that remained constantly capable of unbalancing surprise. Just incidentally, he was about to make five films that are classics of their kind, each of which was entirely different from the others, each of which added something to his range.

The first of them, *The Awful Truth*, is of the sub-genre usefully identified as 'the comedy of remarriage', by the academic critic Stanley Cavell. He argues that as a group (he includes *Bringing Up Baby*, which doesn't quite belong here, *His Girl Friday* and *The Philadelphia Story* from Grant's subsequent work) these pictures, because they are about divorce, or more precisely, the restoration of romantic

order and (and ardor) after the disruption of divorce, represent a significant novelty in the history of romantic comedy, which had heretofore concerned itself with getting a young couple together, whatever the obstacles, for the first time, not the second. This point is to Cavell what the intercostal clavicle is to Grant in *Bringing Up Baby*, a thing pursued with manic intensity and with no awareness of how silly the professor looks in the course of that pursuit or that the funny bone is a reasonable substitute for a clavicle. But no matter. What does matter is that *The Awful Truth* is a kind of tuning fork; by its reverberations one can test the comic pitch of almost any movie on a similar theme – and find them, to varying degrees, just off the note.

For in recounting the troubles that develop between Jerry and Lucy Warriner (Grant and Irene Dunne), when each comes to suspect the other of cheating (he is almost certainly wrong, she is almost certainly right) an almost perfect balance is struck between verbal comedy and farce. The Warriners love each other in the tender, exasperated, bantering way that was established as the proper form of sophisticated address for married pairs by Nick and Nora Charles. They also have a dog, Mr Smith (the same wire-haired terrier that worked in *The Thin Man* series), who provides them with the opportunity to have a goofy custody fight that is devoid of the discomfort one would feel if the dog were actually a child. Mr Smith also provides Jerry with an opportunity to come and go at Lucy's apartment, since he has been awarded visiting rights to the pooch. These visits set up the farce, for Lucy has taken up with Daniel Leeson who lives down the hall with his mother and is played by that paragon of sappy virtue in many a comedy of this period, Ralph Bellamy.

Much foolishness ensues from these triangular encounters. If Dan appears in the doorway to read Lucy a love poem, Jerry is sure to be behind the door, tickling her into inappro-

Grant and his stand-in await a set-up on *The Awful Truth* set. Below, Jerry and Lucy Warriner edge toward their final reconciliation in the movie's beautifully managed last sequence.

priate laughter. If he and his mother drop in, Jerry is sure to be at Lucy's place – and get shoved into the bedroom where another swain has already been stashed, so that a noisy fight can break out between them, ending with a chase through the living room past the dismayed Leesons. If Lucy goes to her singing teacher's apartment Jerry, imagining an assignation, is bound to follow – and stumble disruptively into the genteel recital that is actually going on there. On the other hand, if he is attending a stuffy party at his fiancée's home, Lucy is bound to burst in, pretend to be his distinctly déclassée sister, sing an awful song and then accuse someone in the assemblage of stealing her purse. ('Don't anybody leave this room,' she cries.) What is splendid about all this is that no one overplays their underplaying and that the pace is all of a piece. In the little world that the director, Leo McCarey, created for this film – and he won an Academy Award for his work – everyone is at all times just slightly unbuttoned, so that the stage is always set for the logically improbable. Which means that there is no need ever to descend to the impossible in desperate search of a laugh. It is hard to think of a film that has a steadier, more reliable comic pulse, or of one that more sweetly insinuates itself into memory.

The resolution, which involves a restorative, rebalancing retreat as so many comedies of this era did, to what Cavell calls 'a green place' (i.e., Connecticut) is a little masterpiece of perfect taste. It is the eve of the day on which their divorce becomes final, and Lucy has manoeuvred Jerry into accompanying her then into a situation where he cannot escape spending the night with her. Their separate bedrooms are connected by a door with a faulty latch, the wind has risen, there is a restless cat. That door must swing permanently open ... And it does, powered by perfectly stated and played innuendo.

Grant's work in this film is as neatly balanced as the writing and the direction are.

The secret of his success here and later was well-defined by George Cukor: 'You see, he didn't depend on his looks. He wasn't a narcissist; he acted as though he were just an ordinary young man. And that made it all the more appealing, that a handsome young man was funny; that was unexpected and good because we think, "Well, if he's a Beau Brummell, he can't be either funny or intelligent," but he proved otherwise.'

The art was all based on his developing confidence in himself. He could throw it all away – the humor and the intelligence as well as the looks. He had the art just to be, and no compulsion to prove anything to anybody. He could steal scenes, if he wanted to, but he did not. He had more comic force in *The Awful Truth* than he had in *Topper* (partly because he had a stronger director and more forcefully comic writing to work with), but he was not afraid to pull back into a funny distractedness, a way of talking to other people as if he were talking to himself, and that quality was unique – impossible to find in anyone else in the movies. It was not dissociative, a ploy akin to the slight holding back from full commitment to farce that other actors and actresses – especially the handsome ones – sometimes employed to indicate to their fans that they were not really as undignified or stupid as the role seems to indicate they were. It was certainly not like the good sport air that sometimes developed around a normally more heroic or romantic performer when the indignities started to heap up. No, Grant had a way of being bemused by the lunacies with which he was involved that did not set him apart from them but in the end allowed him to plead innocent on the ground of temporary insanity. 'Look at me,' he seemed to say, 'I'm too intelligent to be doing this. Oh, well. Here goes.' We can identify with that. It's what we are compelled to say to ourselves all the time when events get out of hand.

Distractedness. That was something he did better than anyone. In fact, it became a kind

77

of comic signature for him. But it was only something that curled about the edges of his performance in *The Awful Truth*. It took Howard Hawks to bring it all the way out in him. The occasion, of course, was *Bringing Up Baby*. Who was a leopard. Who belonged to Katharine Hepburn. Who was a spoiled rich girl. Who decided that it would be fun to play around with a palaeontologist as absentminded as Grant's David Huxley. Whose plans to marry a terrible stiff of a girl, and to obtain funding for his museum, and to finish reconstructing the brontosaurus of his dreams, are always getting derailed by Hepburn. There is a terrier in this picture, too, and it is he who steals and buries the intercostal clavicle that gets everybody to chasing around in the middle of the night in Connecticut looking for the fool thing, and the leopard, of course, which has escaped.

Well, it's preposterous. And, in a way, it is Hepburn's picture. As Ferguson said at the time, she is 'breathless, sensitive, headstrong, triumphant in illogic and serene in the bounding brassy nerve possible only to the very, very well bred'. The mess she makes must not seem to be a result of scheming or malevolence, but

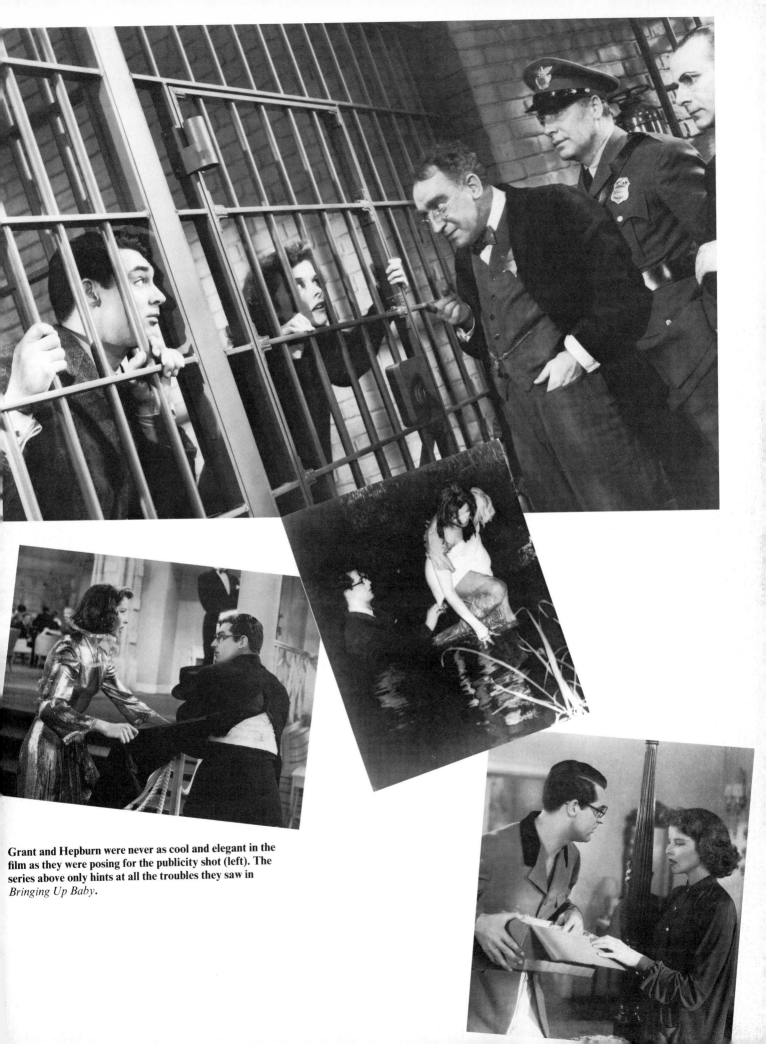

Grant and Hepburn were never as cool and elegant in the film as they were posing for the publicity shot (left). The series above only hints at all the troubles they saw in *Bringing Up Baby*.

A well-publicized *Holiday*. The year was 1938.

KATHARINE HEPBURN ★ CARY GRANT

HOLIDAY

DORIS NOLAN · LEW AYRES · EDWARD EVERETT HORTON · HENRY KOLKER · BINNIE BARNES · JEAN DIXON · HENRY DANIELL

SCREEN PLAY BY DONALD OODEN STEWART and SIDNEY BUCHMAN
FROM THE STAGE PLAY BY PHILIP BARRY
PRODUCED BY ARTHUR HOPKINS
A COLUMBIA PICTURE

PRODUCED BY · EVERETT RISKIN
DIRECTED BY GEORGE CUKOR

the natural outcome of her blithe imperviousness to the normal niceties. Hawks liked to reverse things, to do the simple opposite of what the audience expected of actors, of a comic situation. Hepburn, for example, had previously done a certain amount of noble suffering and a certain amount of romantic dithering, too. He thought the business of making her not merely headstrong, but entirely thoughtless would be funny. 'I think it's fun to have a woman dominant . . .' Hawks would drawl in that off-hand way of his. Same way with Grant. 'Such a great receiver,' the director was heard to murmur years later. Why not take that air of not being all present and accounted for that he had shown here and there in his work and develop it into the core of a comic character.

But it was not in Hawks' nature, or Grant's either, to let the matter rest there. There may be something sympathetic about a nebbish, but there is nothing funny about him. So they

added a certain crankiness to Grant's character – a crabby, exasperated, put-upon quality. After all, the man was a scientist, a rationalist, when he wasn't being distracted. What, logically, would be his response to the sheer impracticality and heedlessness of Hepburn's character when the full import of their consequences to him dawned? Obviously, it would be fuming fury, suppressed only by the demands of propriety (so many of her assaults on him occurred in public, a golf course, a nightclub, her aunt's dinner table, a police station) and politeness (she was, after all, a woman, and he could vaguely remember from childhood that you were supposed to be polite to them, even protect them, as they were 'the weaker sex').

Well, this was splendid. This was even historic. Grant would use this comically-stated balefulness often in the future. It became part of his identity. It was this film that gave rise to

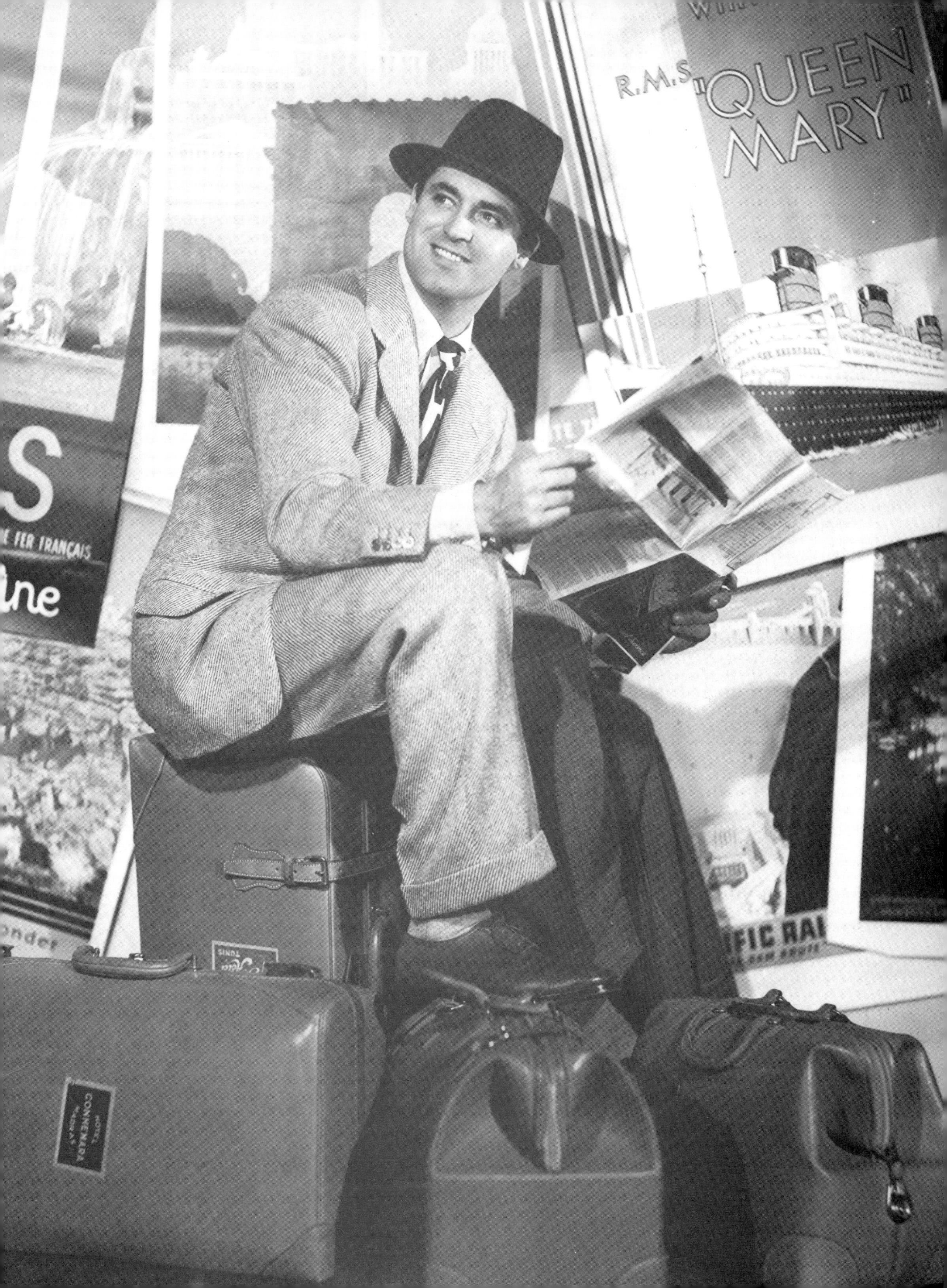

R.M.S. "QUEEN MARY"
FIC RAI

'I find it repulsive when people behave in an unattractive way.' So said George Cukor, and the director was never more faithful to this guiding principle of his career than he was in *Holiday* (1938). And his stars were never more beautiful, or touching, than they were in this adaptation of Philip Barry's elegant and rueful romance, in which Hepburn's childhood playroom became a refuge from the adult world of conspicuous consumption and stodgy social pretense.

Kael's astonishing mix-up of his early screen character with his later one, in that aside from the ones with West, it was the only one in which he could possibly be seen as a male inviting pursuit. Be that as it may the primary importance of *Bringing Up Baby* is as the film in which he established that misogyny that was essential to so many of his best comic effects in the future, that sense that though women could be fun and all, they were – with their strange ways, and even stranger sense of logic – dangerous to one's pursuit of serious male business (work and adventure and, for that matter, just hanging out with the guys). This was, in fact, the great theme of three out of four of his next films, the theme, incidentally, that also bore Hawks' stamp.

First, however, he and Hepburn had other

Director Cukor, Doris Nolan, who played Hepburn's sister (a girl who couldn't learn to live) and Grant on location at Bishop, Calif. for a skiing sequence that did not make it to the final cut of *Holiday*. On screen, Grant and Hepburn never embraced – an intolerable lapse as far as the publicity department was concerned.

pleasures to pursue – more properly, a *Holiday*, with George Cukor. It was one of the two adaptations of Philip Barry plays that this trio would undertake, and it is much less famous and beloved than *The Philadelphia Story*, which came two years later. A case can be made, however, that the first film is the better one, less convoluted and less sententious, though offering neither Hepburn nor Grant roles or a situation quite as complex and interesting to play as the later ones. *Holiday*, however, was a particularly useful film for Grant – presenting him with a down-the-middle role when he needed it. He was not a ghostly fantasy, he was not involved in a screwball situation. He was, in fact, in a very straightforward drawing room comedy, but one which gave audiences a chance to take stock of him, get a fix on this changeable creature who was now so much on their minds. In *Holiday* for the first time he was a surrogate for his democratic audience out there in the theatre, an upscale exemplar of their values.

His Johnny Case is a bright, hard-working lad who meets an enormously rich and socially prominent young woman named Julia Seton while on a Lake Placid vacation. Just how rich and socially prominent he does not discover until he calls on her at the Seton family mansion (trying an experimental yodel in her front hall he discerns a 'bad echo') in order to ask for her hand in marriage. To her father he appears to be a fortune hunter, especially when he informs them that his entire resources consist of $34 and a ticket to a bank night at a Lake Placid movie theater, that his only immediate plan is to take a year or two off to wander and think, get a bearing on what he really wants to do and be. His idea makes as little sense to his would-be fiancée as it does to her father. But her sister Linda (Hepburn) is all in favor of it. She believes the family's joyless spirit, its concern for profits and propriety, crushed her mother's spirit and hastened her death and that her alcoholic brother (superbly

86

underplayed by Lew Ayres) is another victim. Much of the film takes place in their old childhood playroom, their only refuge from the overawing respectability of the family, and Johnny is soon an habitué of that room. And as taken by Hepburn as she is with him – quietly, without so much as the exchange of a kiss or, for that matter, a smouldering or even a lingering glance. The romance is all in the carom-shot dialogue, in a growing mutual respect based on the fact that they are the only people present who are genuinely uninterested in social convention or class obligations. Their words are not funny – there is not a gag line in the picture – but they have sense and sensibility. And there is an easy likeability in the way Grant and Hepburn play together that makes this the most engaging of films.

Indeed, one cannot help but reflect on how much Johnny Case's 'back story' fits Grant's – the young man of natural intelligence and style working his way up to a position where he can appear at ease in the richest of surroundings. This correlation is emphasised by Johnny's continuing relationship with his college professor and his wife (Edward Everett Horton and Jeanne Dixon), who led Johnny gently into the wide world almost as the Penders did Grant; by the fact that his wardrobe is not yet pluperfect (his suit collar does not lie perfectly on his shoulders, for example, and his tailoring sometimes seems a little tight here, a little loose there, bespeaking not the bespoke but the peg): by the fact that Johnny chases the blues not by earnest self-analysis, but by executing a back flip-flop or two – a feat that Grant, the ex-acrobat, manages with perfect offhand aplomb.

More important than what the picture recalls, however, is what it establishes – a centeredness for Grant's screen character, a base, if you will, of simple niceness, of common decency, which none of his previous roles, however charming or attractive they had been, had permitted him to exhibit in so uncomplicated

a fashion. With Johnny Case he gave the audience something it could cling to no matter where he moved in the future.

And the first place he moved was far afield, to India during the British Raj, for *Gunga Din*. Or back to misogyny. The film started out as a Hawks project, with a script by Ben Hecht and Charles MacArthur. This was rewritten by Joel Sayre and Fred Guiol when George Stevens took over the direction, but its structure remains Hawksian in its concentration on the relationship between its three soldier-principals – rough McChesney (Victor McLaglen), smooth Ballentine (Douglas Fairbanks Jr) and crooked, cheeky Archibald Cutter, the Grant character. The plot mostly concerns the first- and the last named trying to prevent the man in the middle from breaking up their gang by leaving the army and marrying a very bland Joan Fontaine. Their largest hope in this regard lies in getting a splendid little war of some sort started – convenient for them that a thuggee cult is about to go on a rampage – in order to distract Ballentine from his romance.

There is, however, a more tender and meaningful relationship in the movie, that between Archie Cutter and the regimental water bearer, Gunga Din, who is played by Sam Jaffe. Archie of course refers us back to Archie Leach, and to Jimmy Monkley in *Sylvia Scarlett* as well. He's a Cockney, but played with a high-spirited broadness that, as much as anything, establishes the larky tone of the picture, which is part send-up, part tribute to the Kipling spirit. But Archie, for all his get-rich scheming, has none of Jimmy's malevolence – he would never victimise friends as Jimmy did. And if his class-sense is also highly developed, it leads not to a hollowing envy of those above him, but to a rough indentification with those below him. Or is Din – who desperately desires to wear a British uniform, and to whom Archie gives lessons in military deportment in his spare time – really below him? Archie seems to think they are both rather in the same pickle – members

89

'Kill. Kill, for the love of Kali.' But it's easier said than done when you are up against the likes of Cutter, MacChesney and Ballantine. Below, opposite, the heroic and cheeky trio have Eduardo Ciannelli, leader of the thuggee cult surrounded, but obviously not yet ready to surrender. This page: bars do not a prison make. Archie Cutter turns the experience into a time of thoughtfulness – mostly about a temple of gold he intends to raid.

of an exploited underclass, each in his way trying to better himself.

This is not a point that is, shall we say, overly stressed in a movie that bustles with well-staged activity (an early small unit combat scene is a high-flung masterpiece of its kind). And it was certainly a point that was generally missed by earnest reviewers of the time who thought that tributes to the spirit of empire, especially jolly boyish ones, were not in the best possible taste. Yet it is Archie's belief that the secret temple of Kali, where the cult of thugs meets, is built out of solid gold, and that a piece or two chopped out of it will greatly improve his lot in life, that causes him to steal McChesney's pet elephant and set out, accompanied by only Din in search of it ('I'm not a soldier, I'm an expedition'). When he sees it gleaming before him, Archie whinnies and jumps like a horse smelling oats. But then it is duty before greed – and what may be the most famous comedy moment Grant ever played. For the temple is soon filled by cult members, who number in the thousands, for a ceremony before their final uprising. In order to distract them so that Din can slip away and summon aid, Grant brazenly reveals himself. His tone and attitude are those of the strongest authority figure Archie Cutter-Leach can remember, a London bobby dealing with say, a gang of street loiterers. 'You're all under arrest ... and you know why! Her Majesty's very touchy about having her subjects strangled. Wrap up your gear. You're coming with me.'

What glorious cheek! The epitome, really, of Grant's round-eyed, bright-eyed flamboyance in these days, the Grant of the joyously amoral Walter Burns in *His Girl Friday* or the deliriously cowardly drama critic, Mortimer Brewster, in *Arsenic and Old Lace*, the Grant who could overplay a scene as sure-footedly as he could underplay one, sailing right over the top into regions of improbability that other actors never penetrated. And could take us along with him on these flights of disbelief. It was this cut-

Man in uniform(s): Grant's career, especially early on, by many a military adventure. Opposite page, clockwise: in full dress on the Indian frontier of *Gunga Din* (1939); in Wellington's army in *The Pride and the Passion* (1957); as an American revolutionist in *The Howards of Virginia* (1940). This Page, also clockwise: As *Butterfly*'s Lt. Pinkerton (1932); in *Operation Petticoat* (1959 – his third submariner); in *I Was a Male War Bride* (1949); in *The Last Outpost* (1935); and in *Destination Tokyo* (1944).

loose, try-anything quality that Hawks loved about him and could liberate in him. And which, sometimes, trying to look back past his later, more controlled and subtle image, we tend to forget.

It was to Hawks that Grant returned once the cult of Kali was stamped out (and poor Din, having perished heroically to warn the oncoming regiment of a deadly ambush has ascended to heaven wearing his coveted British uniform). And it was perhaps only Hawks who could have got him to don the absurd gaucho pants and oversized panama hat – soigné on the way to camp – that he wears in *Only Angels Have Wings*. He is the ramrodder of an air service flying the mail out of the banana port of Barranca, through a mountain pass with the worst weather in the socked-in history of movie aviation to ... somewhere or other. Talk about your Hawksian group! They are old and young, smart and dumb, brave and brave (even the cowardly interloper is only misunderstood). They have built a barrier against the outside world out of overlapping dialogue and Hawks' much-vaunted 'professionalism', which consists of doing whatever job is at hand and not counting the cost, let alone sentimentalising it.

This is a lesson that must be learned by Jean Arthur, who plays Bonnie, a stranded showgirl who falls for Grant, but gets all upset when a young pilot she was about to have dinner with is killed in a crash. She is appalled when his pals sit down and jokily start chowing down, urging her to eat his steak ('What are you going to do with it, have it stuffed?') and teaching her their ways. ('What's the use of feeling bad about something you can't do anything about; he just wasn't good enough.') The problem, besides keeping to schedule so the local government will give the airline a permanent contract ensuring its future, is to turn Bonnie, who has had fair warning about all the other girls who have lost their hearts to the Grant character, ('every third raindrop would fall on one of

them') into an acceptably 'Hawksian woman' (as the phrase now goes) – that is to say, one of the boys. This is no easy matter, for Grant has never been crankier around a woman than he is around Bonnie. For example, one night after he's been out in the rain, mother-henning his boys, he returns to his room to find her trying to make a cheering pot of coffee, an act he greets with a surly question, 'What's all this cooking?' and an equally surly command, 'Stop making a lunch stand out of my room.'

'Jean Arthur half falls apart waiting for him to make a move,' Kael writes of this movie, which is, for her, another prime bit of evidence about Grant's essence as she sees it, which is 'to draw women to him by making them feel he needs them' without coming right out and saying so. But there is something more than a sexually shrewd enticement going on here. What's really up is active resistance. Which resistance is based on an utterly firm belief that women gum up the works in enterprises where men must depend on one another to be undistracted. Grant's character here is not *playing* hard to get; he *is* hard to get. And he is not won until Bonnie, in effect, undergoes a sex change operation, until she proves herself capable of being one of the boys, a flip stoic who suppresses all her womanly impulses to make a fuss about her emotions. Indeed, one cannot help but think that, in considering the movie, Kael is making the same mistake Jean Arthur's Bonnie makes during its course; namely that Grant's sexual indifference must be a ploy, a deeply disguised come-on. It is a common enough female mistake, but a mistake it is. All the come on is in the eye of the beholder. Grant never once plays it, or hints at it.

Partly this is because he is having so much fun playing such flamboyant maleness. Howard Hawks went to his grave proclaiming the 'realism' of the picture, claiming 'Every blooming thing in that is true. I knew the men who were in it [Hawks had been a flyer and knew many of the pioneer aviators when theirs was still a glamorous profession] and everything about it. But it was just where truth was stranger than fiction.' Sure. You bet. Hawks deadpanned it all the way. His *mise en scène* is dark enough for tragedy, which, of course, keeps sniffing jackal-like around the edge of the airport, and the script is replete with the kind of adventure story predicaments that could be resolved by ennobling tragedy. It's just that the dialogue, and Grant's playing in particular, with its marvellously clipped abruptness, keep pushing it toward what it finally became – a parody of the adventure form. For the fact is that Grant generally could not play straight derring-do. When he tried, in *The Howards of Virginia*, for example, or *The Pride and the Passion*, he congealed his awkwardness. The canny Hawks, who always liked a laugh better than a cry, obviously decided to let him go – and to keep his mouth shut about it for ever after. But it was because the picture turned into parody that it received so many puzzled – even outraged – reviews at the time. And why it improves with age while *Ceiling Zero*, the straight version of a similar situation that Hawks made with Cagney three years earlier, dwindles into banality and mawkishness.

Still, Hawks obviously learned a lesson from the picture, which was that Grant was too much of a loner ever to fit comfortably into one of his groups. There is simply no camaraderie in the man. And, for Hawks, no normal sexiness either. He apparently thought that Grant's outstanding handsomeness was an oddity bordering on the grotesque, something that set him for ever apart from the ordinary run of men. Hence what may be the greatest of their collaborations, *His Girl Friday*, the remake of *The Front Page*, in which the part of ace reporter Hildy Johnson, who wants to leave harum-scarum newspapering and settle into domesticity, is played by a woman (Rosalind Russell in this case). And not just any woman, but a woman who was once married to Walter Burns, the toughest, meanest and least tasteful

*His Girl Friday*. **Howard Hawks always liked a twist. And in this remake of** *The Front Page* **he pulled one of his boldest – turning reporter Hildy Johnson from a man into a woman, which gave demonic city editor Walter Burns' obsession with keeping his star reporter on the payroll a splendid new sexual dimension. Rosalind Russell played Hildy, Grant played Burns and, as ever, Hawks played it cool on the set. Below, they check out Billy Gilbert's tale of municipal corruption while one of the corrupters, played by Clarence Kolb, looks on. Center, editor Grant raps out his front page via the phone, while Ralph Bellamy tries to persuade Russell of the virtues of the quiet life. Far right, one of Grant's efforts at friendly persuasion falls on deaf ears.**

city editor Chicago has ever known. Grant plays him dapper – there is a dandy tradition in newspapering. It could be argued that all his vicious scheming to keep Hildy on the job in the press room down at the county court house is an expression of love, making *His Girl Friday* either a comedy of remarriage or even another female pursuit story, though the second interpretation requires a critical leap of astonishing dexterity.

Better to keep it simple. The fact is that Walter wants to reclaim Hildy not as a woman, but as one of the boys, the best pal he ever had. It is a radical restatement of the *Angels* theme, sans loving group dynamics. For Walter never sees himself as part of the clubby little Hawksian group over at the press room; he exploits tham as unmercifully as he exploits everyone else who crosses his path. The fond reminiscences he keeps throwing up to Hildy in his efforts to forestall her marriage (to the ineffable Bellamy) are not of tender romantic moments. They are of scooping the opposition

together, of interrupting their honeymoon for instance, in order to cover a coal mine disaster. If there was something broody in Grant's image in *Only Angels Have Wings*, something that hinted at the lonely soulfulness that can afflict a leader of men (and devastate the woman who observes it) there is none of that here. He is as bold as he was in *Gunga Din*, but bereft of the saving cuteness his Cockney accent imparted to him. Here he is all brass and brashness, fast and loud as he almost never was. His charm is all in his speed, his irresistible energy and single-mindedness. It is sheer authority, as David Thomson says, that becomes 'the brilliant denial of self-destruction, injustice and rampart insanity'. Without this, which takes the form of keeping us laughing constantly, 'outrage and agony would otherwise take over'.

In short, it is a *tour de force* for both Grant and Hawks, a testing of their limits. Could Hawks quick-march a comedy so fast that no one stopped to think about the stench of the sinkholes we were being hustled past (there is the tragic murderer about to face the gallows hereabouts, and more municipal corruption than one dare contemplate)? Yes, he could. And Grant? Could he keep his frenzy concentrated, never let it deteriorate into something we might understand as unattractive desperation? Yes, he could. When he throws out his front page to accommodate news of a murderer's escape and alleged capture by his newspaper, he is capable of ordering Hitler and the war in Ethiopia banished to the comic page, but ordering the story about chickens retained on page one. 'That's human interest,' he cries, and we must indulge him. His single-minded devotion to the awful standards of tabloid journalism is a form of innocence, of otherworldiness, the flip and noisy side of his devotion to *Bringing Up Baby*'s intercostal clavicle, not to be understood as anti-social or mean-spirited. In a way, this was his ultimate test: could he make even charmlessness charming? Yes, he could.

# 5 IDENTITY CRISIS

'HIS GIRL FRIDAY' REPRESENTS A CULMINATION for screwball comedy. With it, the form has been pushed to its outer limits. Indeed, without the lift and drive that Hawks, Grant and Russell imparted to it – a motive force that rocketed it beyond conventional morality – the picture might have stumbled over the edge into sour blackness. For that was really the only direction left to go for comedy that assumed madness not to be an anomaly but a normal, everyday part of existence. Black comedy, though, whatever the virtues of that somewhat desperate and benighted form, was not something for which the times were right or ready. And so the screwball form pulled up short and succumbed to a disease roughly equivalent to the equine ailment known as the wobbles: it began plodding about in ever decreasing circles until it died.

To a degree all comedy in the 1940s suffered as the screwball genre did, though the milder forms were not terminally afflicted. There were several reasons for this. The freshness, the pure delight in the ability to *say* as well as show funny things on the screen began to wane – perhaps inevitably – after the sound film had been established for something more than a decade. The party was running down. Everyone was feeling talked out. Especially the writers. They had been cut off too long from their roots in nervous, verbal, abrasive New York. They were beginning to go soft and over-ripe under the Los Angeles sun. And some of them were beginning to feel guilty about the whole thing. Even those who were not overtly political – and many were not – began now to feel a pressure that was not entirely external to say something significant, important, serious about the state of the world in which they were living so nicely. They had glided through the depression years on the wings of wit and manner borrowed from Broadway in the 1920s. Now with a world war about to begin they were not going to make that mistake again. They would be serious and relevant – and this time their Hollywood bosses would join their more sober peers in encouraging this new weightiness. Washington wanted propaganda from the studios; the Stalinist left, especially active in the Screenwriters' Guild, had decreed a popular front in aid of the war effort. And even comedy could enlist. Sober morals could be pointed perhaps better with a laugh than a preachment. Or so it was said.

It is striking, when we look back now, how quickly the laughter died. Only the last late-bloomer, Preston Sturges, did any work after 1940 that can be considered memorable (*Sullivan's Travels, The Lady Eve, The Palm Beach Story*, for a start). After *Ninotchka* Lubitsch faltered. Frank Capra went off to war to make documentaries. Leo McCarey started doing 'heart-warming' (actually stomach-churning) comedies about adorable priests and nuns. Hawks rounded up his male groups and marched them soberly off to war. We were left with Bob Hope and his platoons of anonymous gag-writers and equally characterless directors. It was awful.

One almost suspects that Cary Grant somehow saw it all coming. Or maybe he sensed that, just as the comic genres in which he had found his first success had reached their limits, he had reached his within them. The range he had staked out was the most spacious any leading man of his type had ever claimed. In the space of four years he had definitively proved that he could do pure fantasy and pure farce, screwball romance and romance of a much straighter variety and, with *Gunga Din* and *Only Angels Have Wings*, adventure comedy both low and high. But still, it was all comedy. Maybe he wanted to write himself an insurance policy against the day the comedy bubble would burst or maybe he simply wanted to prove that the territory he could command was still wider. Maybe he felt he had still not played the person he wanted to become. But for whatever reasons he started reaching out in more sober directions.

In 1939 between *Angels* and *Friday* he

paused to do an interesting, half-forgotten film called *In Name Only*, in which he plays a man unhappily married to Kay Francis – she only wanted him for his money – who 'meets cute' with Carole Lombard on a riding trail in – naturally – Connecticut and in due course seeks a divorce from his wife in order to marry this plain-speaking, fast-speaking girl. Until this point the film has the airs and attitudes of, if not screwballism, then of conventional romantic comedy – pretty people, pretty sets, a glamorous atmosphere – although one keeps wondering where they hid the jokes. But then the atmosphere darkens. After at first seeming to acquiesce in the divorce, the wife reneges – and threatens Lombard (who has a child from a previous marriage and is trying to pursue a career as an illustrator) – with a suit for alienation of affection. The last hope for a peaceful settlement of the issue fails on Christmas Eve – a bit heavy, that touch – and Grant is brought to death's door, by a combination of booze, despair and a slushy night. From which, of course, only the love of a good woman can bring him back. Why, good heavens, one thinks, this is a sudser.

And indeed it is. You can't always tell a movie by its casting. And then one thinks, good for Cary and Carole for taking a chance. And good for the writer for letting the wronged wife deserve to be wronged. And good for Kay Francis for playing her mean as a snake. The result is a better picture than was generally allowed at the time, precisely because it upset both the reigning generic conventions and the reigning moral conventions. And Grant's wary watchfulness is, in this case, extremely well-judged. He *is* a man picking his way through a minefield. And he brings a grace bordering on the gallant to the pathos of the concluding passages. Despite the movie's relative lack of success he had quietly expanded his territory.

He was not so lucky in his other excursions outside the fence in this period. *The Howards of Virginia*, a historical romance, was awful –

*In Name Only*. **Director John Cromwell's dark romance is one of Grant's most underrated films. It is the story of an unhappily married man who meets the woman who can change all that (Carole Lombard) on a riding trail, wins her, then almost loses her when his wife refuses to give him up. It has moments of charm and fun, but it is also one of the most realistic marital dramas of its era – and Grant's career.**

flat and poky, and with Grant looking almost as awkward as he had back in his Mae West days. He seemed to want to be funny, to push the movie along toward some camp ground that only he imagined, but it couldn't be done. Still, it is forgettably bad. *Penny Serenade* is unforgettably so. But because he (and to a lesser degree, Irene Dunne) were so visibly and self-consciously off-cast, he received an Oscar nomination for it. One thinks of the picture as an act of retribution – against him for having so much fun for the past few years, against us for joining in on it.

The story is set up to encourage those feelings. For Grant's Roger Adams begins the film as a journalist of the blithest spirit, a man who commits the unpardonable sins of leaving his wife on their wedding night in order to take up a job as a foreign correspondent in exotic Japan, and of going wildly into debt in order to keep her comfortable. Can't stop the earthquake, though. And it causes not only a miscarriage but some condition that will prevent her from having another child. He knows whose fault all these troubles really are; his for not being a sufficiently sober citizen. And so he buys a small town weekly so he can struggle and scrimp; and earn the emotional right to adopt a baby; and have it grow up to be an

adorable six-year old and play the angel in the school play; and then be carried off by some mysterious disease; and bring the marriage to the brink of divorce; from which it is providentially rescued by the chance to adopt another baby.

The outline is fair to the film; it reduces it to its coldly calculated and manoeuvred basic elements. One understands why Grant may have been drawn to it. There was no dazzle to it or to his role. People could see he was also a serious fellow. It gives him a chance to cross the downside class line as an ordinary American rather than as an extraordinary Briton. He may even have seen in it a chance to play one of the most basic of the sexual conflicts – man as dreamer and wanderer versus woman as nest-builder. Surely, given his life, that would have been of interest to him. But that theme is quickly lost once the tragedies start piling up. And then it is almost as if all concerned became embarrassed by what they were doing. Grant has a scene, for example, in which, his newspaper having failed, he lacks the wherewithal to pass the adoption agency's means test, which means that he and his wife will have to return the child they have been given on a trial basis. He goes to plead for the baby, but he does so in a defeated monotone. And director George

**Reconciliation. In order to arrive at a happy ending with Lombard, Grant would have to pass uncomfortably close to death's door.** *In Name Only* **was released in 1939.**

Backwoods bumpkin and tidewater aristocrat. Otherwise known as Cary Grant and Martha Scott. They overcome the social barriers to find happiness. But *The Howards of Virginia* remained a somewhat ponderous historical saga. Left, director Frank Lloyd, kindly obliges an autograph seeker.

Three camera coverage on a four handkerchief picture. Director George Stevens is at left, Grant and Irene Dunne are separated by the camera covering the master shot. On this page they grimly contemplate the death of their child. *Penny Serenade* (1941) brought Grant his first Oscar nomination and it remains beloved by sentimentalists, but it added little to the gaiety of nations.

Stevens backs off the scene. He's got Grant pinned to a chair in the middle distance and gives him no close-ups. Maybe Grant couldn't cut it emotionally in this scene, or maybe both men thought it would be tasteless to try to cut it. But you can't help feeling that as long as they've gone this far they might as well go all the way. As it stands the scene is self-deprecating. One has to make up a word for it: mawkward. Later in the film, when the child dies, there isn't even a death scene. We learn about it from an exchange of letters, read out on the sound track.

We are in the realm here of career management – a radical change of pace, a sentimental rather than a romantic warming of the image, a bid for prestige. We are perhaps always in that realm when we speak of Grant. His reputation for shrewdness in handling himself, (he had no studio to guide him and there was no agent either) is a legend that the facts bear out. *Penny Serenade* was a hit, and within a few

years he would be operating in the rarefied realm (for the time) of $300,000 a picture. But, for the first time a strategy is obvious, although not for the last time.

And yet one sympathises. Not only with the desire to stretch, but with his overarching problem, the sudden and obvious decline in the quality of what there was to do in his old best vein. Consider the comedies of this period. Right after *His Girl Friday* there had been *My Favorite Wife*, a Leo McCarey project which was turned over to Garson Kanin when the director was seriously injured in an auto accident. It was a reversed *Enoch Arden*, with Irene Dunne as a lady who had been shipwrecked for seven years on an island with Randolph Scott (Grant's room-mate during their early Hollywood years) returning home to find her husband happily remarried, yet still capable of being jealous of her, therefore, doubtless, still in love with her, according to the conventions pertaining in films of this kind. It is a fairly

*My Favorite Wife* **offered the stillsman another opportunity for His Favorite Pose (left). Grant's sometime roommate, Randolph Scott, was the other man in this somewhat strained comedy triangle with Irene Dunne. The director was Garson Kanin – a replacement for Leo McCarey who was hurt in an accident just before shooting started. The year was 1941.**

merry thing, and silkily played by Grant and Dunne. Yet it is not really bouyant in the way that *The Awful Truth* had been. There is a strain on these premises, a feeling that the writers and the director are breathing just a little too hard as they push a very old rock uphill.

And then, after *Penny Serenade*, there was *The Philadelphia Story*. Philip Barry had written the play for Katharine Hepburn when she was involuntarily retired from Hollywood as 'box office poison' – a mysterious label to paste on her, incidentally, since *Holiday*, her last film before her hiatus, had been a considerable commercial success. The play was a hit and Hepburn had bought up the film rights before it opened. As a result, she was able to write her own return ticket to the movies, which included the right to choose the director (Cukor) and her leading men (Grant and James Stewart).

There can be no doubt that Barry did a superb piece of craftsmanship on her behalf. Her image, at the time, was thought to be a little too rarefied for popular tastes; what was needed was to bring her down to earth – down to the earth as close as possible to the plots occupied by sundry girls next door. It was the problem Dietrich had faced and conquered by playing the brawling saloon owner in *Destry Rides Again*. It was the problem they solved by putting Garbo into comedies – wonderfully in *Ninotchka*, less wonderfully in *Two-Faced Woman*. In Hepburn's case the trick was to knock her off her high horse, blunt or anyway democratise her idealism, make her less demanding, more forgiving of people – and, if possible, give her a drunk scene so that that aristocratic diction of hers would become a little slurred. In playing the role of Tracy Lord, that, precisely, is the action of *The Philadelphia Story*. Several of the characters have a go at it – among them the reporter–photographer team from *Spy* (read *Life*) magazine (Stewart and Ruth Hussey) who – despite the invasions of privacy her profession eventually forces them to make – are shown to be good honest working stiffs with decent personal values; a wise, wry uncle (Roland Young) and above all, C. K. Dexter Haven (Grant), Tracy Lord's first husband, now returned on the eve of her second wedding day to try to reclaim her, or at the very least save her from the error of marrying a self-made man who has mostly made himself into a dreadful prig.

It is a wonderful role for Grant. It would be too much to say that his position is to speak up for democracy at Tracy's society wedding. If that were all he was doing he would quickly have had to fall silent in the face of his rival's genuine pluck-and-luck credentials. No, what he is really saying is that lackluster birth is no more a guarantee of basic human decency than good birth is a sure sign of bad values. The aristocracy of the emotionally intelligent is drawn from all classes, all backgrounds, and his truest business is to recruit Tracy Lord for that aristocracy, for which he knows she has the right stuff if she would just let it come forth. In a general sense this is very sly stuff on Barry's part. Writing at the end of the common man's decade, his business was to deflate the outlandish claims made on that literary – political creature's behalf. That a movie making this point could become a success with the very mass audience whose claims to *virtu* it questions, says something either about that mass's tolerant nature or its inability to listen with any degree of subtlety to what was being said.

Much of the credit for this trumpery must go to Grant's playing. He is a sort of an Ariel figure, a busy, devious arranger – of his own happiness, of course and, we do come to believe, of Tracy's as well. His touch is so light, and there is such bemusement in his eyes as he stands back to admire the effects of his schemes, that we can't help but like him. And this despite the fact that he is required to do some very serious speechmaking, not merely about democracy, but about her character. Consider, for example, this response to her charge that his former heavy drinking was 'disgusting'. 'You took on that problem when you

took me on. You were no help there, you were a scold. And my drinks grew deeper and more frequent. She finds human imperfection unforgivable (the line is addressed to a watching Stewart before he turns back to Tracy). You didn't want a husband and a good companion. You wanted a kind of high priest to a virgin goddess.' Let anyone who doubts Grant's qualities as an actor try to think of anyone else who could get away with a speech that floridly accusatory (and self-pitying) and still retain an audience's good regard. Indeed, one doubts even if Grant could have managed it had he not long since established his credentials as a man with (shall we say?) a very realistic view of the opposite sex and the tributes it can exact from the male. There *is*, always and for ever, a war between the sexes – but Grant is one of the rare actors in films who acknowledges it, even when he is distinctly the pursuer as he is here, even when the script makes no direct mention of this prevailing condition.

So the speech works, the whole film works – thanks to him, thanks to the slick professionalism of everyone connected with it. And yet one does not embrace it. There is, between it and *Holiday* (which after all, took the same theme of privilege versus democracy in a less convoluted way) a distinct falling off. There is a loss of waywardness in both dialogue and characterisation. The former has lost the light bounce, that was its former glory. And there is something a little too schematic about everyone in *The Philadelphia Story*. They all too much represent idea and positions, and one misses, for example, the mysteriously maimed younger brother of the earlier film, the authentically damaged – and therefore authentically human and authentically cautionary – note he brought to it. Beyond that, one agrees with Gary Carey, who wrote a sharp little book about Cukor's films. He found that in the process of 'humanising' Hepburn, Barry actually seems to be splitting her in two, separating out (and putting down) some of her best and most

individual qualities – 'her aristocratic demeanor, her intelligence and her inner-directedness' – in order to force up her warmth and charm. In her best roles – and *Holiday* was one of them – 'it is the harmonious combination of both sides of her character that makes her so winning'. Another way of putting it is that it is her very difficulty that makes her singular. And any work that does not encourage us to take her or leave her as she gloriously is must inevitably seem to be pandering to the crowd's, the mass media's worst impulse, which is always to reduce complexity to simplicity, high spirits to sentimentality.

Something similar happens to Grant in the picture. After the prologue, in which – Hepburn having snapped one of his golf clubs over her knee – he gives her a furious, and furiously comic push in the face, he never has a true Grant moment. He never gets to whinny like a horse or turn a handspring, dance a jig or wear a dress. He never even gets to talk too fast. As he plays a man to both manner and manor born, one senses for the first time that the process of his becoming what he is playing is beginning to take hold. After all, he is now only a couple of years from marrying his own Tracy Lord, the Woolworth heiress, Barbara Hutton.

But we are spared nothing in life – not even if we are movie stars. And so Cary Grant, having skipped blithely through the depression, his social conscience entirely unburdened, came at last to concern, involvement, the big issues: in *The Talk of the Town* (1942) and *Mr Lucky* (1943). They are not bad. They are better, for example, than *Once Upon a Honeymoon* (also 1942) in which he was a newspaperman trying to get a stripteaser out of Europe ahead of the advancing Nazi hordes, or *Once Upon a Time* (1944) in which he was seen as the manager of a dancing caterpillar, two travesties which a merciful memory now almost entirely veils. By contrast, *The Talk of the Town* and *Mr Lucky* are both well made. If they ground his spirit

113

The wedding that ends the *Story* (left), the aftermath of the fight that begins the process of working out its resolution (below). Frank Capra (right) visited the set.

they ground it gracefully, with a certain intelligence. In the first, co-written by Irwin Shaw and Sidney Buchman, with George Stevens directing, he is Leopold Dilg, who has been a nuisance, a classroom cut-up in the town where he was born. Somewhere along the line his anarchical spirit was politicised. ('Some people write novels. Some people write music. I make speeches on street corners.') One does not quite believe it – Cary Grant on a soapbox! – but since the film does not actually require us to contemplate this depressing spectacle, we can perhaps ignore the naggings of disbelief. In any event, he has been falsely accused by the town's leading citizen – the owner of its principal factory – of arson and murder, and the film opens with him escaping jail and taking refuge in a country house owned by Nora Shelly (Jean Arthur) which she is preparing for a new tenant, Prof. Michael Lightcap (Ronald Colman), a legal scholar and civil libertarian – Justice Douglas with an English accent – who is moving in to write a book in peace. We are on the brink, here, of violating one of madcap comedy's most sacred conventions. The green place is about to be polluted by politics, the disorders of the world are about to intrude upon the retreat, the purity of which was essential to the restoration of bedevilled perspective. There is, however, some nice knockabout as Arthur tries to keep Grant hidden from her visiting professor, some nice irony when, her secret

115

Portrait of a radical: Grant as Leopold Dilg, (left) more a small town cut-up than the dangerous subversive the story tried to make him out to be. Above, Ronald Colman pauses on his way to the Supreme Court to win Grant's case for him – and to learn that the law has a human side. Jean Arthur gives Grant his just reward (right). The interesting script was by Irwin Shaw and Sidney Buchman – the former fresh from his anti-war plays on Broadway and his memorable *New Yorker* short stories, the latter fresh from *Mr Smith Goes to Washington* and *Here Comes Mr Jordan*. The director was again George Stephens – his third and last collaboration with Grant.

*Once Upon a Honeymoon.* **Journalist Grant tries to spirit stripteaser Ginger Rogers out of wartime Europe with the Nazis in hot pursuit. This 1942 comedy-adventure was one of director Leo McCarey's less happy inventions.**

revealed, the two men take a liking to one another, and begin discussing the gap between the law as theory and the law as reality – the idea being largely to disabuse the professor of his innocence on the latter point. That's good populist stuff. And his involvement in Dilg's case, which includes doing a little rough-and-ready private detective work before taking it to court, gets him out from behind his books and will surely make him a better, more humane Supreme Court justice, which is what he becomes at the end of the picture.

Grant makes a good fugitive. He can use his natural wariness, his alert passivity, to advantage. And sometimes when the talk is thick we can see that he is not paying attention to it. What does all this chat have to do with the fact that the cops are on his tail, and have previously demonstrated but small interest in defending him from a lynch mob? It is right and good that his mind wanders from abstractions to survival. Archie Leach's would have. If he has a problem here, it is not with his playing but with his image. That he is a man of mischief has been long-since established; that he is a man of the serious left, a true radical capable of inflaming a whole community, no, that does not quite go down.

*Mr Lucky* is, on that ground – but only on that ground – shrewdly calculated, for it does not discover Grant committed to anything. His Joe Adams is at the outset a gambler with a boat, a floating casino which he anchors offshore to conduct his business, with an eye fixed exclusively on the main chance. Nor is his history an open book. 'Nobody ever knew what he was – except tough,' says his friend, narrating the story after it appears that the criminal had died a heroic wartime death, torpedoed at sea. Especially since the lighting is *noir*ish, it seems that what we are about to witness is Grant's *Casablanca*, the story of a shady soul regenerated by popular front idealism. But as we move into the tale, the mood brightens and the pace quickens. Looking for a respectable

cover, Joe aligns himself with a war relief organisation managed by a group of society ladies, and is soon enough smitten by its deputy director, Dorothy Bryant (Laraine Day). We are now suddenly in the country of romantic comedy – society dame and a mug from the wrong side of the track (or docks) falling for each other. Whereupon we fall over into the land of the screwballs. The ladies set Grant to work knitting in a window where passersby can see him. It is a great Grant moment – a drag scene without a drag outfit, and charmingly goofy. Not long thereafter, Joe and Dorothy head in the classic manner to the green world – Dorothy's family home in the country. We expect a romantic peacefulness to fall over their scrappy affair. Wrong again. When she proposes marriage, he fires back the opening barrage in what will quickly turn into class warfare: 'To people like you, folks like me are animals ... We're so bad and you're so *very* good ... You look through me like I was a dirty pane of glass...' and so on. Then, however, a priest tells him tales of children suffering under wartime hardships and the filthy pane is cleansed; one can see through it now to a heart of gold. A plan by some of Joe's mob pals – to steal the take from a gambling concession Joe is managing at a charity ball managed by Dorothy's organisation – is foiled by him and ... It is by this time like a breathless tale made up by a child, all hasty twists and turns, eager to please at any cost.

It is amazing. It is weird. It defies description. What is this movie? What is its main line of business? It never makes up its mind. And that reflects its curious beginnings. The original story is by one Milton Holmes, who was a tennis pro at a club where Grant played. He approached the star with the basic idea and the actor got the studio to buy it and assign Holmes to turn it into a script. Given his inexperience, however, it was thought prudent to bring in a more seasoned partner – none other than Adrian Scott, who would soon enough

*Mr Lucky*. **Or the screwball spirit develops a social conscience – with a little help from** *film noir*. **Somehow, it all worked better than it sounds. Grant played the gambler whose love of a good society woman (Laraine Day) causes him to abandon his greedy ways in order to enlist in the fight against fascism. Of course, you have to learn to knit before you can take up arms. Which Grant did (overleaf) in the movie's funniest scene.**

find a larger fame as one of the Hollywood Ten. There must be one of the great unwritten farces in this situation – the tennis bum and the gentlemanly communist sitting down to collaborate on a comedy for one of the world's most glamorous stars.

And one in which he was taking a personal interest. For there is a third element of interest in the film – a minor but palpable autobiographical note. Grant occasionally uses Cockney rhyming slang (most notably 'Lady from Bristol' which means 'pistol' in the argot). There are references to a povery-stricken past and of a mother going hungry so that her child would be fed. His character is also given a rationale for not entering military service, which was something of a touchy subject for Grant who, despite his age – he was close to forty – seems to have felt guilty about not entering the service. 'I had my war,' says Joe, 'climbing out of the gutter. I won that war. It's the only war I recognise.'

It might have been a recipe for disaster, this unlikely collaboration between a man who had been a servant in the upper class world that madcap comedy had purportedly represented, a product of that world (which the Amherst-educated Scott was) who had somehow managed to identify his interests with those of the working class, and an actor looking for ways to breathe life into the genre that had given him his life as a star. But it was not a disaster. If *Mr Lucky* is hardly a great movie it is not a bland one or a stupid one either. It is in fact more memorably dislocating than many of Grant's smoother and better loved movies. At least on the subject of class it is, for example, more abrasive, perhaps more emotionally honest, than something like *The Philadelphia Story*.

But of course, it is critically a dangerous movie. The mixture of personalities in the writer's office, the resultant mixture of moods and motives in the film itself, have such a tempting historical symbolism – that one per-

122

haps finds it more interesting than it really was. But if one must quarrel against claiming too much for the picture, this much is certain: it is an apt and convenient place to mark the end of an era, an end to the giddy delights of a kind of movie making for which we lost the taste for seeing, then the knack for making.

Grant lost something almost immediately – his main line. He would, in time, find another one, though never one as interesting, as quirky, as full of surprises for us, for himself, as the comedies of this period had provided. In the short term he was – no other way to put it – 'interesting'. He went from *Mr Lucky* to *Destination Tokyo*, as the commander of a submarine. It is a good solid war adventure arguably the best of the Up-Periscope breed, certainly Grant's most successful effort to play a completely straight hero. His Captain Cassidy is stalwart, intelligent and sober as a judge. There were at least a dozen men in Hollywood who could have played him just as well. Then he did his fable about the dancing caterpillar, *Once Upon a Time*. And then he did *None But the Lonely Heart*, over which one must reluctantly pause because it meant so much to him.

His friend Clifford Odets adapted the screenplay from the novel by Richard Llewellyn, and Grant saw to it that Odets got the chance to direct it. It is a very solemn, very lugubrious movie that seems to have represented two different things to each of its two principal creators, making a grand total of four – or three motives too many for making a movie. For Odets, the Group Theater's star, the leading voice of the American theatrical left in the 1930s, it was a chance to establish himself solidly in Hollywood (he had had but one screen credit eight years previously and he had never been given a chance to direct). It was also a project he thought could be made to honor honorably his political line. For the central figure, the Cockney Ernie Mott, was, as an opening voice-over informed us, a man looking 'for a free, noble and better life in the

second quarter of the twentieth century', but unable to realise his natural talents (they seem to be mainly for philosophising) because he was always being pushed back into a life of petty crime and rascality by poverty. Through him Odets would, from the very citadel of escapism and materialism, make a major assault on the social determinism which capitalism enforces on people. And, incidentally, get in a few kind words for the popular front, for when war comes – at the end of the movie – a bomber flying by is seen, incredibly, as a symbol of regeneration.

For Grant, of course, this was his first 'serious' role, an image-blaster of the kind that frequently wins Academy Awards (indeed, he did get another nomination, losing the Oscar to Bing Crosby who had done him one better by switching from crooning to the priesthood in McCarey's *Going My Way*). But if Grant and Odets had analogous career hopes for the picture, their conceptions of it were entirely at odds. As Manny Farber pointed out at the time, we never witness that search for the 'free, noble, and better life' the narration gasses about, or any other persuasive connection between the modest events presented on the screen and the large general points that Odets wanted to make. Ernie may indeed have been a searcher, but when we first pick him out (no easy task considering the murky light and wacky angles Odets favored, not to mention the fog he kept pumping into his set) his wandering days are over. What we will see him do is come home to mother, engage in a life of petty crime, and see her through a final illness (though Ethel Barrymore, in the role, looks entirely robust physically and does not seem exactly downtrodden spiritually by her life of poverty, either). There are obviously points of similarity between Ernie Mott and Cary Grant. The actor had surely known what it was to be poor, and to want a better life. His sympathy with a man who could not break free as he had been able to must have been lively. Then, too,

125

Grant was instrumental in getting playwright Clifford Odets the chance to direct his first feature, his own adaptation of Richard Llewellyn's *None But the Lonely Heart*. June Duprez played a girl friend who was no better than she should have been, while Barry Fitzgerald occasionally joined him in the shadows of London's East End for some confused, but glum, philosophizing. It was the kind of picture that won the good opinion of people who harbored toney aspirations for the movies, but does not wear awfully well.

he knew what it was to be estranged from his mother, and perhaps had his guilts on this matter, too. For though they had been reunited, and he supported her as handsomely as she would permit, his visits to her were perforce few and far between, and perhaps without the full wish-fulfilling reconcilement that he was able to permit Ernie to enjoy in the film.

So. Good intentions. Earnestness. These qualities mark Grant's performance, too. But it is too careful – or possibly insecure, and what might have lifted the picture rather adds a final deadly burden to it. Ernie is, in the last analysis neither a better nor a worse person than Jimmy Monkley in *Sylvia Scarlett*. There is no reason, except sober and sobering aspirations, why he could not have been a feisty victim, or even a gallant one, instead of the whiner he was. With energy and wit, Grant might have made us care for him. A bitter irony here: the one role Grant valued most highly is also the one role he entirely misjudged. He would not pass this way again.

*Arsenic and Old Lace*, which he had made for Capra in 1941, but which could not be released until the Broadway show closed in 1944, now came out. There are those who think his Mortimer Brewster was also miscalculated: too frenzied in its cowardice, too manic in its pursuits of laughs. It is surely not his most urbane performance. And yet there is something courageous in his outrageousness. It is as close as he ever came to giving a Hawksian performance for any director but Hawks. And it works. It is mostly his energy that permits the film to burst its stage boundaries, and turn it into a moving picture. And anyway, what's a man supposed to do when he finds bodies buried all over his maiden aunts' house? Arch an ironic eyebrow? Hone a Wildean epigram on the subject? No, let those big brown eyes pop and roll! Let the voice rise into the boy soprano range!

Anyway, it beats standing around in Cole Porter's dinner jacket, blandly pretending that

the composer's domestic tragedies – if such they actually were – stemmed from workaholism, not homosexuality, which was the basic conceit of *Night and Day*, a musical revue pretending earnestly to be a biography. Grant has one nice, cut-loose scene – in which he labors under the misapprehension that Linda, the lady he loves, may have married while he wasn't looking, and that she may even have had a child. Or two. Or three. Or ... But as they chat in the park close on a dozen children are blandly introduced to him, and he does one

Grant was Ernie Mott, a Cockney everyman who was turned to crime by grim determinism. One of the characters who did the turning was Milton Wallace. Ernie's capacity for the better things was demonstrated by his love for his mother, Ethel Barrymore.

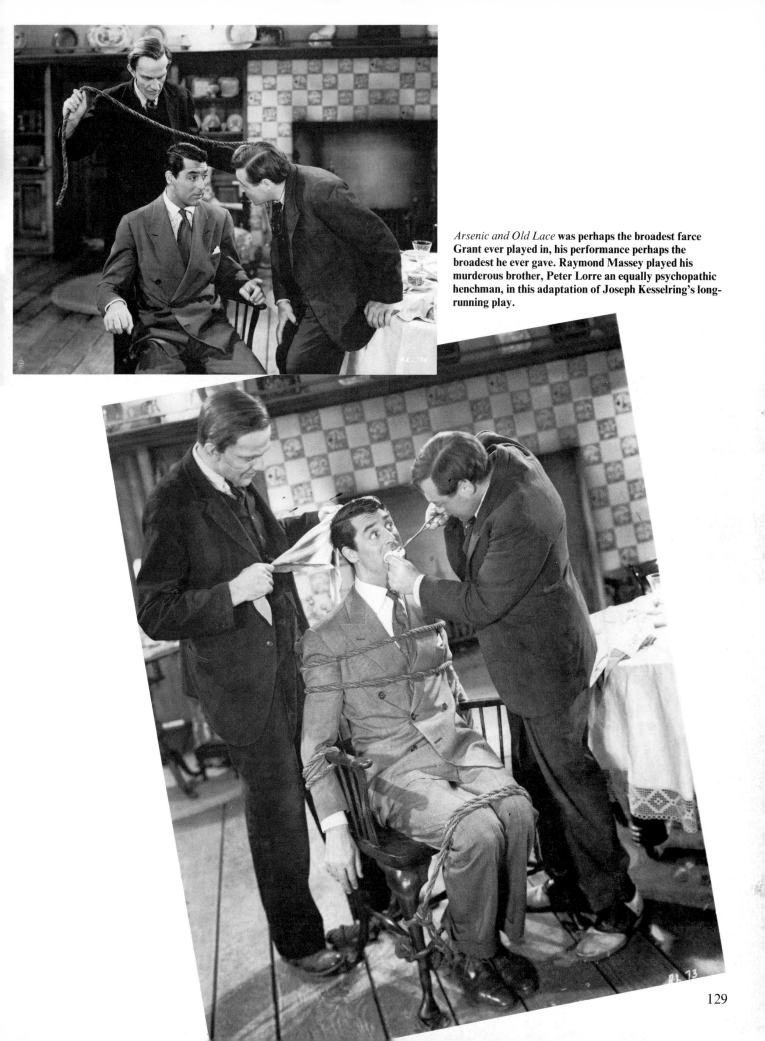

*Arsenic and Old Lace* **was perhaps the broadest farce Grant ever played in, his performance perhaps the broadest he ever gave. Raymond Massey played his murderous brother, Peter Lorre an equally psychopathic henchman, in this adaptation of Joseph Kesselring's long-running play.**

This is not the sort of situation in which drama critics like Mortimer Brewster expect to find themselves when they are off-duty. In their sweet little ways Mortimer's aunts (played by Josephine Hull, seated, and Jean Adair) were as deadly as brother Jonathan. Something's very amiss with that elderberry wine their guest is about to drink (below).

great double-take after another – rising up the scale from dismay to horror to disgust, a *tour de force* for the actor as reactor. Until he discovers that the lady works in an orphanage and that these children are her charges, not her kith. On the whole, he is not as sappy as the picture. He maintains a certain fastidious dignity.

But what are we talking about here? What are we looking at? The year was 1946. It was only six years since he was the finest movie actor in the world, maybe in history. What was that phrase? 'He can be attractive and unattractive simultaneously; there is a light and dark side to him, but whichever is dominant the other creeps into view...' Yes. Where have they gone, those dazzling, those mercurial alternations? Why, suddenly, do we seem to be confronting nothing more than a plain, basic leading man – smooth and professional, entirely likeable and entirely bankable, but for the moment without distinction or individuality, except that which trails after him out of his past?

It may be that, in his forties, with so much accomplished already, he lost his taste for risk, became conservative. It is not an unknown phenomenon. And in the years ahead there would be well-documented tales of good roles inexplicably turned down – the James Mason

t ought to be good. None
f it's true.' Thus Cole
orter on *Night and Day*,
ie movie version of his
fe. Grant had the
legance to convey the
ian's spirit, but the rest
f the movie did not.
lexis Smith played Mrs
orter, whose chief
omplaint against her
ian was not that he was
homosexual, but that he
vas a workaholic. The
ilm's best comic turn was
he scene (right) where
he pretended that a
roup of orphans she was
ending were her own
hildren. Grant's
astidiously expressed
orror at the tastelessness
f excessive breeding was
joy to behold.

part in *A Star Is Born*, the William Holden part in *The Bridge on the River Kwai*, Henry Higgins in the movie of *My Fair Lady*. But one suspects the problem lay elsewhere, outside himself. He had conducted his career and his life boldly, with small thought for the conventional wisdom, and there would yet be choices – actor's choice, that demonstrated the courage to go anywhere he needed to go for a laugh, a surprise, something memorable. But a man cannot impose his courage on his times. And those times in the movie business – the late 1940s, the 1950s, the early 1960s – were not brave ones. It was a period first of semi-documentaries and pop Freudianism, then of Cinemascope and the pre-sold property, of Biblical epics and Doris Day's endlessly imperilled virginity, an age of ponderous blandness. The quickness and craziness of the Hollywood which had so suited Grant's spirit was suddenly gone. Being, as we know, an intelligent and adaptable survival artist, he would find ways to prosper in the new Hollywood. Indeed, he had been the great pioneer of what was now to become its prevailing business style – independent production – and perhaps better than any star of his generation he would find and burnish an image that would carry him entirely undiminished

through this period. But he would find only one film-maker with a spirit that somehow reverberated to his, someone who would bring out in him not only the old unpredictability, but a new dangerousness.

Alfred Hitchcock had also risen out of the English lower middle class, partly also by imagining a character for himself and then learning how to play it. He was as much a loner, and far more of an eccentric than Grant, and of course saw in the actor precisely the qualities that reflected his own vision of life – a romantic and humorous surface with dark undercurrents running beneath, always ready to burst forth. All of Hitchcock's anxiety – and he was as much the poet of anxiety as he was the master of suspense – was based on this unpleasant awareness that things were never what they seemed, that disorder always lurked below our treasured middle-class orderliness. All his movies were based on setting up a chain of circumstances that would bring his characters to an acknowledgment of that awareness. There was not a single leading male figure in any Hitchcock movie that Cary Grant could not have played.

He began with him as early as 1941, with *Suspicion*, in which he played an obvious

fortune hunter and a famous womaniser who takes an improbable interest in country mousey Joan Fontaine, keeps failing his promise to reform and take a job, and then appears to be planning to murder her for her money. Grant is wonderful in the role; he is not quite smooth, so his comical high spirits make the threat he poses to the woman more than a mere menace. It brings the film close to the grotesque. His heightened playing underscores the film's basic question, keeps forcing us to wonder if we are seeing him objectively or are we seeing him through her increasing paranoid eyes?

The film's suspense derives entirely from that ambiguity. In the book on which it is based, and apparently in the early drafts of the screenplay, Grant's character was indeed a murderer, and it must be said that that implication is inherent in scene after scene, so much so that we do not fully believe the film that was finally released, in which the woman's suspicions are proved groundless. Hitchcock would later say that the studio had insisted on this resolution, because the public would not have accepted Grant as a criminal. He would also say that he felt that the twist ending, the sudden banishing of carefully-built anxiety, was more surprising and satisfying than the one for which logically he had prepared us. There is something in this, and there is so much fun and energy in the film (and in Grant's performance) that one is almost able to avoid the edgy, cheated feeling it leaves one with. But not quite.

What is significant about *Suspicion* is that, for the first time one really feels the dangerousness of a charm as seductive as Grant's. It was perhaps hinted at in *Sylvia Scarlett*, but the world of that film was so remote, and his character so exotic, that it did not menace as it does here, where Fontaine (who is very good and vulnerable) makes us feel its sexy lure, its ability, helplessly, to enthral.

But given what he did between 1941 and 1946, there was no opportunity, aside from *Mr Lucky* to develop and exploit this aspect of his

135

Menace in the milk. In *Suspicion*'s most famously suspenseful moment (far left) audiences were encouraged to think hard about just what Grant might have put in Joan Fontaine's glass because Hitchcock hid a softly glowing light in it. Below: She should have known he was no good the minute they met – and he had to borrow first-class train fare from her.

persona. His work in this period had the effect of cutting off the top and the bottom of his range – he was never as funny as he had been in the Hawks comedies either – confining him to the middle. It was Hitchcock, in 1946, who restored him to full vitality. *Notorious* is one of the director's most sinuously romantic films. It has in its *mise en scene* the moodiness of *Rebecca*, for example, but Ben Hecht's script, with its first-rate espionage story, and its unexpected twists of characterisation, has a delicate, and delicately building, suspense that does not grab at the viewer, but, rather, bewitches with an almost hypnotic seductiveness.

As Devlin the counterspy Grant is cool, brusque, competent – with an almost sadistic edge of cruelty about him. At the start it is clear that his assignment is distasteful to him – recruiting and running an amateur, and a woman at that. And what a woman she is. Ingrid Bergman's Alicia is not only the personally loyal, if politically disapproving, daughter of a convicted Nazi spy, she is also a nymphomaniac and an incipient alcoholic, unstable to the point of explosiveness. And emotionally needy, pathetically so. 'Why won't you believe in me, Devlin – just a little bit,' she begs at one point. And our shock at seeing Bergman violate her previously pristine image, degrading herself in her need, is, like Grant's charmless manipulativeness, one of the things that makes this movie so superbly unbalancing. She is, in Kael's terms the pursuer, he the pursued, but in the movie's own terms that is less significant than the neurotic force-field it wants to set up between them.

In effect, Devlin is forced to become her lover in order to calm her down enough to do her job, which is to insinuate herself into the home and circle (in Rio de Janeiro) of Alexander Sebastian, who is played by Claude Rains, in one of that impeccable actor's most delicious roles, as the only master spy in the history of the genre who is hag-ridden by his mother (yet another piece of pathology to reckon with). His circle is, of course, really a ring – a spy ring, in search of sources of uranium for Hitler's atomic bomb.

What Devlin does not count on is that he will fall genuinely in love with Alicia. Or that Sebastian will ask her to marry him. And that there is no way out of the match if she is to complete her mission. What neither she nor the audience had counted on is Devlin's neurosis, which now comes to the fore. He thinks she accepts the situation too easily; her attitude fits all to well with what he knows of her earlier promiscuity; and with all the fears and suspicions of women in general which she had almost made him forget. He turns petulant as a jilted schoolboy, reaching levels of mean-spiritedness that from any leading man would startle an audience, but which from Cary Grant are almost devastating. Hitchcock and Hecht have now stripped him bare of his protective image as they previously did Bergman. The resolution of *Notorious* requires not just the restoration of moral order, but the rebalancing of psychological equilibrium as well. And what dark intensity this brings to the normally routine process of sorting out a spy drama's strands. One feels that if one of the Brontës had attempted an espionage story it would have turned out something like this.

With *Notorious* we come closer to the heart of Grant's darkness – as close as he would allow us to come. There were two decades left to his career, but only once – and then again for Hitchcock – would he risk anything like this exposure. Something assuredly was lost by the

There was something neurotic in the need of Bergman's character for Grant in *Notorious*. And vice versa. Theirs were among the hungriest embraces recorded on film until that time. But his rescue of her (right) from the clutches of Madame Sebastian (Madame Konstantin) and her son (Claude Rains) was classically scary Hitchcock.

reticence. And yet one can scarcely blame him. Self-revelation is a terrible trial for anyone; it is especially so for an actor, whose instrument is his person; most of all for an actor like Grant, who so carefully and deliberately created a screen character that was as much a fantasy to him as it was to his audience, in which he could comfortably hide himself, or whatever of himself – that is to say, the Archie Leach who had been – that still existed. Besides, there was no demand on him for such exertions. The movies of the next decades had small requirements along these lines, and they could be adequately handled by the new generation of actors who defined an actor's work (and worth) differently from Grant and his generation. And the public? It was entirely content with what he offered it – adoringly so. If anything they preferred to dream on about him undisturbed. It was a preference he could easily – more easily than ever, as it turned out – oblige.

141

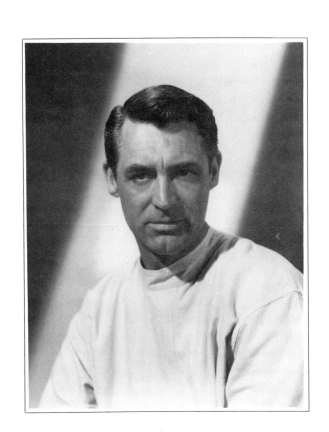

# 6 BEDAZZLING

DO WE – DOES CARY GRANT – OWE THE FINAL, boldly simplifying, boldly vulgarising resolution of the identity crisis that plagued him throughout the 1940s to Sidney Sheldon? Before he became the best selling author of glamour-trash, Sheldon toiled in decent, not to say deserved, obscurity as a screenwriter with no impressive credits, until in 1946 he wrote something called *The Bachelor and the Bobby-soxer*. It was his little contribution to solving a more serious identity crisis, namely the creation of a screen character for the adolescent (by this time late-adolescent) Shirley Temple, something that would restore to her that uncanny hold on the public which she had enjoyed as a nymphet a decade earlier. In this, like everyone else, he failed. Grown up, she stubbornly remained just another bland, snub-nosed cutie, a star who had reversed the usual process and become a starlet. But for Grant, Sheldon casually produced a miracle.

His story idea was this: she was to develop a typical adolescent crush on a dazzling older man, manoeuvre him into a compromising situation with her, one that actually puts him into jeopardy with the law, and then, given a choice by the judge (who is Myrna Loy, who is also her sister, who will also ultimately provide the mature love interest for him) he must either serve a jail sentence for impairing the morals of a minor or accept another kind of sentence, that of being her date until she grows tired of him and starts looking with favor on swains of more suitable age and status.

Well, yes, put just that way the situation does seem a tiny tad improbable, but it did at least restore Grant to the country of sheer goofyness from which he had been absent since he had helped bring up baby; any movie that gets him into a three-legged race with Rudy Vallee and a bunch of adolescents can't be all bad. Still it is dubious that Sheldon deserved an Academy Award (which he won for this picture, joining the long list of writers who had been made to look better than they were by the way

Grant read their lines) just for thinking it up. What he may have deserved it for was the brilliant thought of having Grant appear on screen as – and have him talked about by the characters as – an effortless lady's man, to appear in film fictions as what he had become in fact over the past decade to his bedazzled female beholders – a perfect dreamboat or, to borrow a phrase from the most bedazzled of them, 'the man from dream city'.

He had never appeared as such before – never. Of course he had always got the girl, if there was a girl around to be got, but there was nothing remarkable about that – the leading man was supposed to receive that just dessert. It was, rather, the manner of his achieving this reward that was here commented upon. Everyone else seemed to have to try too hard. Most of the time Grant seemed merely to stroll comfortably and unruffled towards his objective and it would fall into his arms. Sometimes he didn't even seem to stroll towards it – just by it, looking the other way. As with his roles, so it was with his movie career, as a hard-working show-biz denizen like Sheldon could not have helped noticing. Even now, as Hollywood entered its most anxious days since the coming of the talkies, with a vast reorganisation of the very method of doing business getting under way under the impress of television and the consent decree, the terms of which required the studios to divest themselves of their movie theaters, Grant just kept ambling gracefully, graciously along, agentless and advisorless, at the top of the popularity polls, no matter what he did or didn't do (and, as we have seen, there had been no apparent agony in his choice of material in this decade). In Hollywood terms, it made no more sense than the uncanny hold he seemed to have over the women fans. It was as if he had something about him that no one else had, some secret resource, some mysterious gift of the gods, some magic. . .

Click. Rattle-rattle goes Sidney Sheldon's typewriter. Grant is addressing a class at Shir-

144

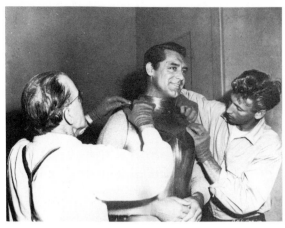

The Bachelor and the Bobby Soxer (left) strike an agreeably silly pose to publicize an agreeably silly movie. Shirley Temple played the smitten teenager, Myrna Loy her older sister. The film has a certain historical importance as the first in which Grant's former-implicit capacity for bedazzlement was turned into a manifest quality. Right, he is helped into his shining armor for a day-dream sequence in which he appears all aglimmer to the adoring Temple.

he possessed, certainly nothing he had cultivated or worked for. (Oh, really? 'I pretended to be somebody I wanted to be, and I finally came to be that person.') And so long as he played it that way, as a gift, men did not resent him the way they did some other stars. They might envy him in a wry, almost self-amused way, but they did not resent him. Those few who did, those who circulated the rumors about him being homosexual, well, he is on record as saying they did him a favor. By so doing, he has said, they demonstrated their own insecurity and also piqued women's curiosity about him, with the result that she 'zeroes in on my bed to see for herself'. How very Cary Grantish. How magical. And if he had really been homosexual that would have been all right, too. We would have been out of the realm of the merely magical and into that of the purely miraculous. Splendid, really, to be alive and witness to so prodigal and ironic a transcendence: the most enrapturing star in the history of the movies, turns out to be gay.

But if Grant, bless his shrewdness, never himself seemed to summon up the magic, if he always let it happen in the eye of the beholder, his scripts and his directors were encouraged to enhance it. He was not quite the innocent bystander in the process that he pretended to be. If he wasn't always his own *de facto* producer he certainly had free choice of his material, and approval of everything significant that happened on his sets. And he became cautious in his managerialism. Scripts were re-written so that the burden of exposition was taken from him, and his great gift for listening, reacting, could be exploited. It is said that he worried greatly about the fragility of his charm, and avoided all situations which might imperil it. Astonishing isn't it, considering how all-encompassing, how redoubtable it seemed to us watching. Often as not, through some bit of dialogue, some trick of camera or lighting, it was suggested that this natural charm now had taken on near-supernatural roots.

ley Temple's high school. She is gazing rapturously at him. She starts to daydream. The man in the business suit disappears. There appears before her a knight in shining armor. She is blinded by his glow and glitter. How simple. How perfect. And for ever after, that which had been implicit, unspoken in his screen character, would be explicit. People would talk about it in the pictures. They would visibly react to it. It would be his manifest quality, like Jack Benny's tightness or Marilyn Monroe's breathless promise of availability. It was as plain as the nose on Durante's face. People had to react to it before they could react to anything else about him.

He played it smart. 'Everybody wants to be Cary Grant' he once said, '*I* want to be Cary Grant'. Or words to that effect. He never got pushy about it. It was, he seemed to suggest, one of life's unearned increments, something he was as surprised as anyone else to discover

In the very next picture, *The Bishop's Wife*, 1947, as Dudley, a guardian angel, he literally descends from heaven to set things to rights between an over-worked, and perhaps too materialistic, churchman (David Niven) and his wife (Loretta Young) who longs for their old life – struggling, perhaps, but warmed by affection. She, of course, half falls in love with their unearthly visitor, but who would not? He can trim a Christmas tree with a flick of the finger, reorganise the files with a casual gesture, turn her into an Olympic level skater simply by guiding her around the ice. The magic here is quite literal – a whole picture infused with the spirit of Sidney Sheldon's knight-in-armor scene. There is a supreme – one almost wrote 'divine' – logic in Grant's extra-terrestrial status. It was always part of his essential screen character that he rarely had any visible means of support or any discernible roots. He was always as much the man from nowhere as the hero of any western, always as much the man from no discernible place as the man from dream city (though of course it is arguable that they are one and the same thing). Therefore, why not be a heavenly messenger? If there is such a place surely one of its pleasures is the chance to lose your Bristol accent.

Be that as it may, the film as a whole functions for this phase of Grant's career as *Holiday* functioned for him in the earlier phase; it established the base – in this case the fantastical base – from which he would work for the rest of his time on the screen – almost two decades. It suited him in his maturity, this outsider, effortlessly entering people's messed up lives in his heavenly tailoring, an ironic eye cocked on these mortals, his every gesture and expression implying a knowingness that would have been awesome if he did not so casually throw it away. And the miracles are not all of physical rearrangement, either. There are moral re-arrangements to be made, too. In *The Bishop's Wife* his eyelights shine bright, highlighting the burning quality of his gaze as he wills the other characters to be their best selves. They don't notice, but we do, in the audience, and we get this message: style is, can be, a moral quality. This, too, is a kind of transcendence.

In *People Will Talk*, 1951, writer–director Joseph L. Mankiewicz secularises Dudley. Noah Praetorious is a gynaecologist, a daring occupation for the movies at that moment, but what better one for a man with Grant's supposedly perfect and instinctive understanding of women? And there is more to him than that. He has his own clinic where he practises what we might now call holistic medicine. And he teaches at the university. And lectures informally to friends and colleagues on ethics, morals and the condition of the modern world. (People may or may not talk, but Joe Mankiewicz always did – too much and too sententiously in the liberal-secular-humanist vein.) Praetorious also saves souls. His servant is a murderer he has saved from the gallows. He marries a pregnant patient (Jeanne Crain) to prevent her either from committing suicide or having an abortion. He also flawlessly conducts the university symphony orchestra. He has actually moved up – from angel to saint. And it is one of the rare movies in which Grant is actually unlikeable. He cannot overcome the smugness of Mankiewicz's writing, and that quality adheres to him. But yet, if the conscious intention is to play upon the magic that has accreted around him, the hope was, perhaps, that the opinions being offered would acquire the status of holy writ. But even casting Cary Grant as Moses does not make Joseph L. Mankiewicz Jehovah.

In Alfred Hitchcock's *To Catch A Thief*, 1955, a cat burglar is terrorising Monte Carlo – or anyway that portion of it that keeps its jewellery in the drawer of the dressing table. The police, naturally are baffled. Though up on a picturesque hilltop lives Cary Grant, pretending he's John Robie, the retired jewel thief. The new crimes match Robie's *modus operandi*. And since no one has seen him lift a laboring

A wide-open range, or don't fence him in. The delirious days were now behind him, but there was scarcely a Grant film of the later years did that not offer him at least a moment of exuberant foolishness. For example: as the heavenly-harpist of *The Bishop's Wife*. Or in *Charade's* justly celebrated shower sequence. Or doing his high-flung highland fling in *Indiscreet*. Sometimes he got a whole movie in which to strut smartly his best stuff. As when he overcame his natural antipathy to heights in order to play John Robie, the cat burglar in Hitchcock's *To Catch a Thie*

Sometimes the stills are funnier than the movie. A case in point: Howard Hawks' *I Was a Male War Bride*, which cast Grant as a French officer being smuggled home in drag by his WAC bride (Anne Sheridan). The English title (poster, right) didn't improve matters for a funny idea nervously executed. How about *Bringing Home Baby*? *Her Boy Friday*? *Only Frenchmen Have Things*?

finger in a long time he is a prime suspect (that's the trouble with having no visible means of support and no rooted loyalties – it makes unimaginative people suspicious). Crankily Grant descends from his mountaintop to set things to rights, restore peace and order. He is, if anything, crabbier, meaner and more misogynistic than he was for Hitch in *Notorious* – but so much so that he is over the line into comedy. Two women will pursue him – the daughter of an old colleague from the Resistance, who turns out in the end to be the burglar, and, famously, Grace Kelly. The two ladies have a wonderful cat fight over him in the water near a float, and Grant has one of his best scenes, swivelling his head from one antagonist to the other, like a spectator at a tennis match, saying nothing but vastly enjoying being the cause of all this female hostility. One likes the scene better than his later, more overtly unpleasant scenes with Kelly: 'What you need I have neither the time nor the inclina-

tion to give – two weeks with a good man at Niagara Falls,' and a declaration that his interest in her is 'the same as I have in horseracing, modern poetry and women interested in weird excitement'. At heart, in fact, this is a thoroughly nasty-minded film, with Kelly managing to seem both a prig and a nymphomaniac, and Grant being at heart a sadist (at the film's end he actually tortures a confession out of the thief). But that is precisely why it is so fascinating. Hitchcock's style here is so glamorous, especially in the way he sets up his shots of Grant, so that they always bedazzle, that one's attention slides right past the ugliness. It is as if the old master deliberately wanted to see how many sins his star's now well-established image could cover. All of them, as it turned out.

In *An Affair to Remember*, 1957, we meet him aboard ship, on the first night of an Atlantic crossing: Nickie Ferrante, international playboy, and internationally recognised as such. As he makes his way along the passageways, in his perfect dinner jacket, people stop and stare and do double takes – as any of us might do if Cary Grant came strolling across our path. He is almost languid in his self-assurance, and his self-amusement. He knows the stir he's causing. What star does not? But he is enjoying it. We are out of the realm of acting here, and into the realm of personal appear-

Talking pictures. Grant gave writer Richard Brooks his first chance to direct and Judy Garland visited the set of *Crisis* in 1950. Grant played a brain surgeon whose medical ethics come into conflict with his political conscience when he must try to save the life of a South American dictator. He still had scalpel in hand the next year when he played a humane gynaecologist for Joseph L. Mankiewicz (right) in *People Will Talk*. Below, one of the many lectures Grant gives in the movie.

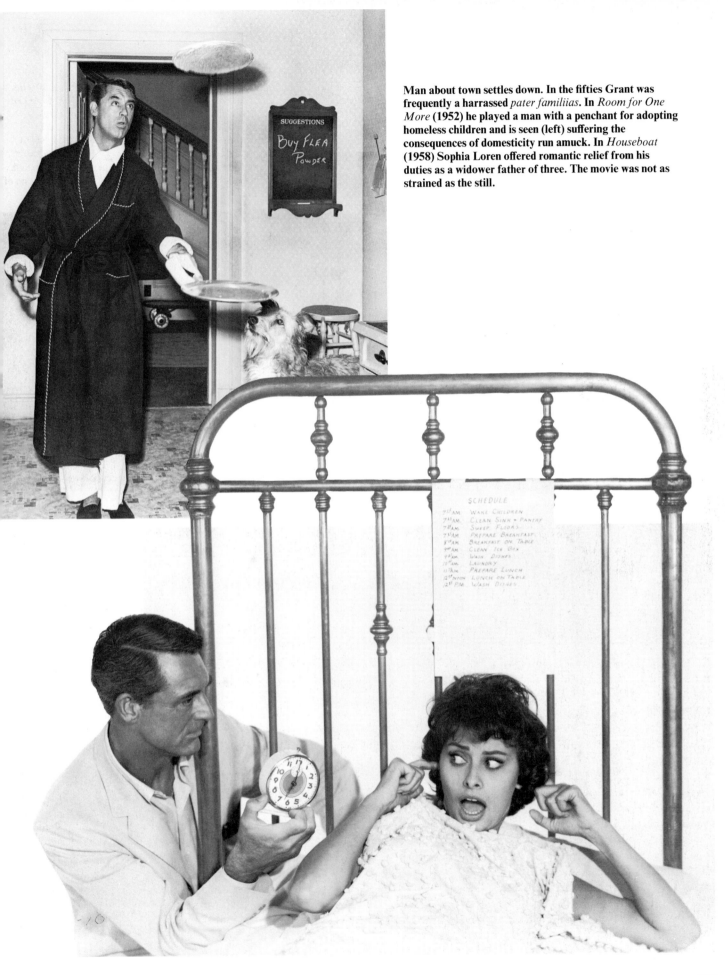

Man about town settles down. In the fifties Grant was frequently a harrassed *pater familiias*. In *Room for One More* (1952) he played a man with a penchant for adopting homeless children and is seen (left) suffering the consequences of domesticity run amuck. In *Houseboat* (1958) Sophia Loren offered romantic relief from his duties as a widower father of three. The movie was not as strained as the still.

SUGGESTIONS

Buy FLEA Powder

SCHEDULE
7ᵗʰ AM   WAKE CHILDREN
7ᵗʰ AM   CLEAN SINK + PANTRY
7ᵗʰ AM   SWEEP FLOORS
7ᵗʰ AM   PREPARE BREAKFAST
8ᵗʰ AM   BREAKFAST ON TABLE
9ᵗʰ AM   CLEAN ICE BOX
9ᵗʰ AM   WASH DISHES
10ᵗʰ AM  LAUNDRY
11ᵗʰ AM  PREPARE LUNCH
12ᵗʰ NOON  LUNCH ON TABLE
12ᵗʰ PM  WASH DISHES

ances. And the director, Leo McCarey (remaking one of his previous hits, *Love Affair*, with Grant cast in the old Charles Boyer role) is aware of it. He is giving us more of what he knows we want – another chance to drop dead at the star's feet. Leo McCarey lest we forget, made *The Awful Truth*. Cary Grant, lest we forget, made it with him. How far we have come since those days. How far the wretched McCarey has yet to go in this film, into excesses of sentimental Catholic piety, including kid choirs and warmly human priests. Grant at least steps fastidiously around all that. (There is a wonderful moment when, called upon to cross himself, he does three-fourths of the gesture – but ends up adjusting his necktie).

In *Indiscreet*, 1958, Ingrid Bergman is tired. She has just returned from a trip. She may have a cold coming on. No, she doesn't want to go out to dinner with her sister and her brother-in-law. Or meet their eligible bachelor friend. And then: angle up – Bergman's POV. There is a man in the doorway. He is backlit. He seems to glow, to radiate masculine power perfectly deployed. You can't even clearly discern his features. But that tailoring, that stance, so casual and yet so commanding! She sees Grant almost as Shirley Temple saw him in his suit of armor. And the message is clear. A woman, even a mature and sensible woman, can now see him only one way – through adolescent eyes. Having gone past acting to appearing, we are arrived now at a kind of common-consent apotheosis, an unspoken agreement, democratically arrived at, that the only permissible response to him is bedazzlement.

The rest is a blur. *Every Girl Should be Married, Room for One More, Dream Wife, Kiss*

154

*Monkey Business* **(1952) returned Grant to absent-minded professorship – and represented at least a partial return to their pre-war form for the partnership with Howard Hawks. The latter always counted himself lucky that he made his two pictures with Marilyn Monroe before fame rendered her too insecure to meet his highest value, professionalism. She had a small part and a big scene with Grant.**

*Them for Me, Houseboat, Operation Petticoat, The Grass Is Greener, That Touch of Mink, Father Goose, Walk Don't Run.* The titles are all alike and one has trouble, without a trot, remembering which one belongs with which hazy memory. Sit-coms and domestic coms, sex coms and Service coms – mostly they were pleasant, and Grant was never less than a gracious professional in any of them. Many of the characters he played in these films were identified with the middle-class professions; they

were doctors and ad men and other sorts of up-scale businessmen. This was extremely shrewd. America in the 1950s was much preoccupied with the folkways of The Man in the Grey Flannel Suit, with the welfare of his soul, or if not that, then with the question of whether or not he could actually be said to have one. The social commentators saw in this figure's alleged concern for regularity and steadiness and in the paltry qualities of his ambitions, cause for alarm, evidence that the spirit that had made the country great was being drained away in an increasingly corporatised state. For Grant to invest this character (beginning perhaps with 1948's *Mr Blandings Builds His Dream House*) with some of the magic that inevitably trailed behind him from his previous roles was really rather decent of him – made people feel a little bit better about their humdrummery to see a fellow like Grant caught up in it but still looking fine and being mildly (if no longer wildly) funny about it. In a sense he humanised the statistics by showing the humorous side to the harrassed husband-father-provider – often through the loss of dignity that frequently involved a reversion to childishness. The audience that had grown up with him and who had now entered the middle class (and middle age) were obviously more numerous than the social critics and pleased to see Grant so gently and affectionately and understandingly portraying their problems and foibles on screen. And to be demonstrating, in the process, that the business of getting a little older and a little richer need not be an unmitigated horror. He was, in his way, a relief from the dour moralists. And, in his way, he was testifying to the truth of his own experience. He had met sober, sensible Betsy Drake in 1948, she had worked with him in a couple of movies, and then they married. She was, it seems, a settled and settling kind of woman. She directed Grant's attention to psychology (she later became a practising psychologist) which helped him fit into an era of life with self-contemplation. Their quiet life was like that which

Siren's song. Sophia Loren has offered pleased public testimony to Grant's prowess as an off-screen lover, a breach of his privacy that, for once, elicited chuckles instead of fuming from the man. He visited her on the set of *Two Women* at Cinecitta in 1960 and draped an avuncular arm around her sister Maria (below). They met on *The Pride and the Passion* when they co-starred with Frank Sinatra in Stanley Kramer's ponderous tale of hauling a ponderous gun through the Spanish countryside during the Napoleonic Wars. They smiled gamely enough at the premiere (below), but the picture was a failure.

his screen character sought and suited the quietism of the historical moment. If one is less than enthused about his screen roles of this period, looking back on them, it is only because they are, in their nature, so much less exuberant than the Grant roles of his best (and our better) years.

Of course, the pace would be deliberately changed from time to time. As early as 1949 Howard Hawks tried to revive the old screwball spirit with *I Was a Male War Bride*, a funny conceit that was desperately unfunny in execution, the only visibly frantic search for laughs in which those two cool professionals ever involved themselves. Three years later they did better with *Monkey Business*, in which Grant reprised his absent-minded professor characterisation from *Bringing Up Baby*. The movie was strained but still funny (any movie that involves Grant with chimpanzees and Marilyn Monroe can't be all bad either). Certainly it was more entertaining than *Crisis*, in which he was a brain surgeon (another magical figure, but this time taken even more seriously than Mankiewicz's gynaecologist was) forced to operate talkily on a South American dictator. And *The Pride and the Passion* in which Grant appeared ludicrously, glumly as a British officer fighting the Napoleonic wars in Spain. It so dismayed him that he announced his retirement after it was released (he stayed

*An Affair to Remember* **was released simultaneously with** *The Pride and the Passion* **in 1957 and was, if anything, more painful. Remaking his 1939 hit,** *Love Affair* **Director Leo McCarey (looking on as Grant and co-star Deborah Kerr face the music) mixed in the sugar-water religiosity of two of his other hits –** *Going My Way* **and** *The Bells of St Mary*. **The result was literally God-awful – tasteless** *and* **sexless.** *Kiss Them for Me* **(opposite, top) fecklessly involved him with Jayne Mansfield (and Leif Erikson) and was no improvement.** *Indiscreet,* **actually involved him very discreetly with Ingrid Bergman – and adulthood – again.**

*North by Northwest*. **Never did Hitchcock more brilliantly use comedy, romance and thrills to hide his true theme – the sadistic degradation of pride – than he did in this film. Below left on location. Below right evil begins the process of revenging itself on charm. Or anyway, giving it a lesson in humility.**

away only a year). Toward the end, in *Charade* (directed by the graceful Stanley Donen with whom he formed a producing partnership in these years) there was an attempt to see if his magical qualities were of any use as a secret weapon in counter-espionage. He appears more as Audrey Hepburn's guardian angel than as her lover (though he becomes that too) when she becomes an innocent victim of a somewhat preposterous conspiracy. It is not at all bad – as good a Hitchcock film as anyone not named Hitchcock ever made.

But it was the work of the genuine article that is the only Grant film that stands out in memory in this period. *North by Northwest*. Or Hitch's revenge. Roger Thornhill is Cary Grant seen through envious instead of adoring eyes. He is rich, and getting richer in his glamorous advertising job. His tailoring is impeccable. His success with women smugly implied. But in Alfred Hitchcock's world everyone is guilty of something, and Roger is guilty of carelessness and superficiality. He's flip about his women; he steals other people's cabs in the rush hour; he's just a little too smooth and soulless. And then the spies mistake him for a

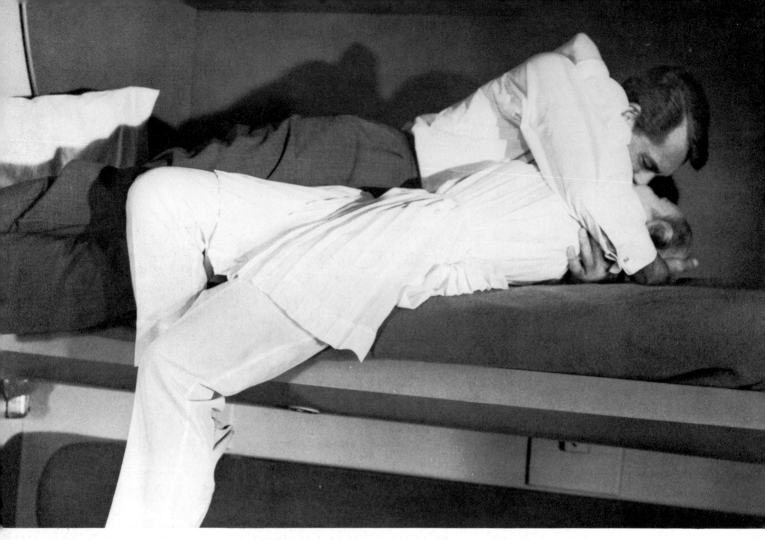

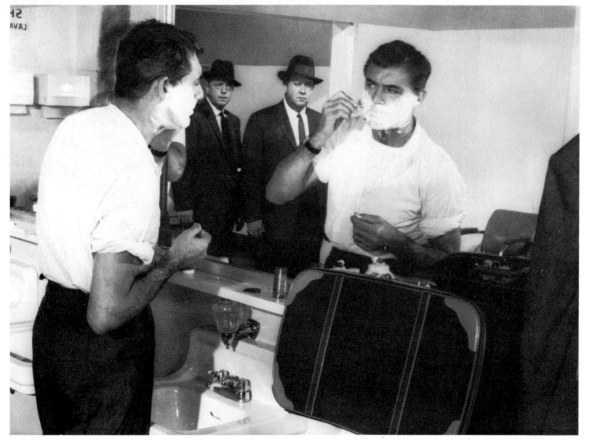

Of Grant's many adventures in *North By Northwest* only one of them – with Eva Marie Saint – was any fun for him. The rest were nothing but nasty surprises.

CIA agent they were supposed to abduct. He escapes them, but only at the price of becoming a wanted man. He must run and hide – in the classic Hitchcock manner – from both the police and the representatives of evil.

But Roger is clever. He is good enough to keep ahead of everyone, and the film's great scenes – Eva Marie Saint's seduction of him on a train, the aeroplane attack on him in an open field; the auction house scene, where he deliberately calls attention to himself with crazy bidding – it's really a screwball scene – so that all attention is focused on him and his enemies cannot murder him there and then; the chase on Mount Rushmore; these are now legends. What we may forget in the sheer rush of all this bravura film-making is how often, how confidently, Roger thinks he has figured out everything, how often, how confidently he proceeds on those judgments – and how every time he turns out to be dead wrong. The structure of the film is to humanise him through mortification, to keep chipping away at his smug self-confidence until finally he has expiated his original sin of superficiality, and knows in his bones, in his soul, how fragile our illusions are, how thin the skin of our social order, our civility is. The point of *North by Northwest* is, paradoxically, to destroy Roger Thornhill's arrogant innocence, strip him of the adult's protective layering, artifice and illusion; to return him to the anxious state of a lonely child in a darkened room; to ask him to reimagine himself and reimagine the world; to make of him, if you will, an Archie Leach.

The extremes of age! What a plague they are! How much more pleasant – and stop to think of it, how much more tasteful – not to inflict either on strangers – not the anxieties and regrets of youth, not the fears and infirmities of age. After *North by Northwest* such dangerous country would be skirted. And if one regretted the loss to the art of acting, one was also grateful to Cary Grant for stopping in his fit and prosperous (and heaven knows, extensive)

His character's name, with its biblical overtones – Peter
Joshua – suggests that Grant was heaven-sent to protect
Audrey Hepburn's bereft Regina in *Charade*. At any rate,
there was something magical in him once again in the best
of his 1960s films. Right, Audrey Hepburn wonders how
he manages to work a razor into his chin cleft. His director
was his partner in Grandon films, Stanley Donen, and this
was the last of four films they made together.

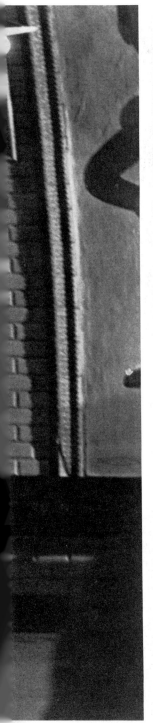

middle age, fixing it in our minds permanently, leaving us with such a pleasant image. No more than he ever was on screen did he become a nuisance. He was not a political bore. He was not a crusader for odd diets or religions or ways of life. He did not turn up on commercials for geriatric products or as a spokesman for conglomerates. He had to make no comebacks from alcoholism or drug addiction or serious illness. He had his marital afflictions, (his relationship with his fourth wife, Dyan Cannon, was particularly testy, but she gave him a daughter, on whom he happily doted), but on the whole they were managed quietly; they were not the subject of hilarity on the talk shows. As far as public life was concerned, he became a grey ghost, a blur on the paparazzi's lenses and caught thus, in motion, he reminded us of his former self, his former lightsome self. Refusing to succumb to age's great trap – tediousness – refusing to pander to youth or to curiosity, he finally became what long years ago he set out to be – a gentleman. Of the old school.

His more recent pictures were, in the United States at least, the ones most often played on television, and it was through them – by and large – that he became best known to the younger generations. To them, oddly enough, he became an exemplar, the progenitor of something that has come to be known of lately as 'The New Man'. That is to say the man who eschews the rough, insensate *macho* (their contemptuous word) ways of the typical American male, especially as he had been presented on the screen. His attentiveness to women, his lack of sexual insistence, the gently knowing and patient irony of the way he confronts them – his lack of hot-bloodedness – commended his screen character to the young women who liked to think of themselves as feminists. And the bright young men – and many not so young – learned the wisdom of emulating him. In the long run, it gets you further. But this was, perhaps, an unearned, unexpected, possibly unwanted, increment as far as Grant was concerned. One could not imagine him consciously desiring to be a weapon in the latest confrontation in the war between the sexes – quite out of character. One could only imagine him arching an eyebrow in that quizzical way of his, and offering his comment in the form of a puzzled, faintly irritable snort. If he took any pleasure in this new state of affairs it would have been over the evidence it offered that his conduct of his later career was better calculated than even he imagined.

But the final chapter in his story is as yet unwritten. History, as opposed to false nostalgia, or contemporary social commentary, is still clearing its throat, making its judgements based on all the evidence. It is mindful that

film has this curious property generally unanti-
cipated by men and women of Grant's generation and earlier. It lasts. It hangs about. It
preserves one's youthful follies, one's
unguarded, sometimes uncalculated, sometimes miscalculated, sometimes entirely glorious follies. In his last years Grant was heard
to say, defensively, 'The stuff's tinny now.' He
was also heard to say he could not remember
anything about actually doing those parts. The
most he would concede about his former self
was, 'He was very immature compared with
me. But I quite liked him.'

Yet what could he do about it? The rest of us
can bury our pasts, pretend they were otherwise
than they were. A screen actor never can. And
though he may tend and burnish his late image,
it cannot outlive the journalism that records
these efforts. And one tends to think that most of
Cary Grant's late films, pleasant though they
are, will not long outlive him either. A trick will
be played on his mortality by his chemical and
mechanical immortality. It will persist in
throwing up on screens of unpredictable sizes,
shapes and venues, images of a young man
intent on becoming someone else, a quick,
quick-changing young man with an odd way
of cocking his head when he listened, an odd,
unplaceable accent when he spoke, a young
man who had an uncanny way of drawing
people to him, and an equally uncanny way of
seeming somewhat dismayed when they came,
a silly young man who was yet morosely
dismayed about what he would never have
called the human condition but which still
made him rather snappish. Dudley, the angel
in *The Bishop's Wife*, once had cause to
remark: 'The only people who grow old are
people who were born old to begin with.' In
that case, that young man cannot ever grow
old. He – this great actor's creation – is truly
ageless. And for that miracle we may be truly
grateful.

# FILMOGRAPHY

**1 This Is the Night** △
DIRECTOR Frank Tuttle
SCENARIO Avery Hopwood from *Pouche* by Rene Peter and Henri Falk
DIALOGUE George Marion Jr
PHOTOGRAPHY Victor Milner
CAST Germaine (Lily Damita); Bunny West (Charlie Ruggles); Gerald Grey (Roland Young); Claire (Thelma Todd); Stephen (Cary Grant); Jacques (Irving Bacon); Chou-Chou (Claire Dodd); Studio Official (Davison Clark)
RUNNING TIME 80 minutes
RELEASE DATE 8 April 1932
PRODUCED BY Paramount Publix

**2 Sinners in the Sun** △
DIRECTOR Alexander Hall
SCENARIO Vincent Lawrence, Waldemar Young and Samuel Hoffenstein from a story *Beach-Comber* by Mildred Cram

PHOTOGRAPHY Ray June
CAST Doris Blake (Carole Lombard); Jimmie Martin (Chester Morris); Claire Kincaid (Adrienne Ames); Mrs Blake (Alison Skipworth); Eric Nelson (Walter Byron); Mr Blake (Reginald Barlow); Mrs Florence Nelson (Zita Moulton); Ridgeway (Cary Grant); Grandfather Blake (Luke Cosgrove); Grandmother Blake (Ida Lewis); Fred Blake (Russ Clark); Mrs Fred Blake (Frances Moffett); Louis (Pierre DeRamey); Emma (Veda Buckland); Lil (Rita La Roy)
RUNNING TIME 70 minutes
RELEASE DATE 13 May 1932
PRODUCED BY Paramount Publix

**3 Merrily We Go to Hell** △
DIRECTOR Dorothy Arzner
SCENARIO Edwin Justus Mayer from *I, Jerry, Take Thee, Joan* by Cleo Lucas
PHOTOGRAPHY David Abel
EDITOR Jane Loring
CAST Joan Prentice (Sylvia Sidney); Jerry Corbett (Frederic March); Claire Hempstead (Adrianne Allen); Buck (Skeets Gallagher); Charlice (Florence Britton); Vi (Esther Howard); Mr Prentice, (George Irving); Dick Taylor (Kent Taylor); Damery (Charles Coleman); Butler (Leonard Carey); Housekeeper (Milla Davenport); Baritone (Robert Greig); Minister (Rev. Neal Todd); June (Mildred Boyd); Stage leading man (Cary Grant)
RUNNING TIME 88 minutes
RELEASE DATE 10 June 1932
PRODUCED BY Paramount Publix

**4 Devil and the Deep** ▽
DIRECTOR Marion Gering
SCENARIO original story by Harry Hervey
PHOTOGRAPHY Charles Lang
CAST Pauline Sturm (Tallulah Bankhead); Lieutenant Semper (Gary Cooper); Commander Sturm (Charles Laughton); Lieutenant Jacques (Cary Grant); A Lieutenant (Gordon Wescott); Hassan (Paul Porcasi); Mrs Planet (Juliette Compton); Mr Planet (Arthur Hoyt); Mrs Crimp (Dorothy Christy); Hutton (Henry Kolker)
RUNNING TIME 70 minutes
RELEASE DATE 12 August 1932
PRODUCED BY Paramount Publix

## 5 Blonde Venus △

DIRECTOR Josef von Sternberg
SCENARIO Jules Furthman and S. K. Lauren based on a story by Josef von Sternberg
PHOTOGRAPHY Bert Glennon
EDITOR not credited
CAST Helen Faraday (Marlene Dietrich); Ned Faraday (Herbert Marshall); Nick Townsend (Cary Grant); Johnny Faraday (Dickie Moore); Ben Smith (Gene Morgan); 'Taxi Belle' Hooper (Rita La Roy); Dan O'Connor (Robert Emmett O'Connor); Detective Wilson (Sidney Toler)
RUNNING TIME 85 minutes
RELEASE DATE 16 September 1932
PRODUCED BY Paramount Publix

## 6 Hot Saturday △

DIRECTOR William A. Seiter
SCENARIO Seton I. Miller, adapted by Josephine Lovett and Joseph Moncure March from Harvey Ferguson's novel
PHOTOGRAPHY Arthur L. Todd
CAST Ruth Brock (Nancy Carroll); Romer Sheffield (Cary Grant); Bill Fadden (Randolph Scott); Conny Billop (Edward Woods); Eva Randolph (Lillian Bond); Harry Brock (William Collier Sr.); Mrs Brock (Jane Darwell); Camille (Rita La Roy); Annie Brock (Rose Coughlan); Ed

W. Randolph (Oscar Appel); Aunt Minnie (Jessie Arnold); Archie (Grady Sutton)
RUNNING TIME 73 minutes
RELEASE DATE 28 October 1932
PRODUCED BY Paramount Publix

## 7 Madame Butterfly ▽

DIRECTOR Marion Gering
SCENARIO Josephine Lovett and Joseph Moncure March from a story by John Luther Long and the play by David Belasco
PHOTOGRAPHY David Abel
CAST Cho-Cho San (Sylvia Sidney); Lieutenant B. F. Pinkerton (Cary Grant); Lieutenant Barton (Charlie Ruggles); Goro (Sandor Kallay); Yomadori (Irving Pichel); Cho-Cho's Mother (Helen Jerome Eddy); Cho-Cho's Grandfather (Edmund Breese); Mme Goro (Judith Vasselli); Suzuki (Louise Carter); Peach Blossom (Dorothy Libaire); Mrs Pinkerton (Sheila Terry)
RUNNING TIME 86 minutes
RELEASE DATE 30 December 1932
PRODUCED BY Parmount Publix

## 8 She Done Him Wrong △

DIRECTOR Lowell Sherman
SCENARIO Harvey Theu and John Bright
PHOTOGRAPHY Charles Lang
EDITOR Alexander Hall
CAST Lady Lou (Mae West); Capt. Cummings (Cary Grant); Serge Stanieff (Gilbert Roland); Gus Jordan (Noah Beery Sr.); Russian Rosie (Rafaela Ottiano); Dan Flynn (David Landau); Sally (Rochelle Hudson); Chick Clark (Owen Moore); Rag-time Kelly (Fuzzy Knight); Chuck Connors (Tammany Young); Spider Kane (Dewey Robinson); Frances (Grace La Rue); Steak McGarry (Harry Wallace); Pete (James C. Eagle); Doheny (Robert E Homans); Big Bill (Tom Kennedy); Bar Fly (Arthur Housman); Pal (Wade Boteler); Mrs Flaherty (Aggie Herring); Pearl (Louise Beavers); Jacobson (Lee Kohlmar); Mike (Tom McGuire)
RUNNING TIME 66 minutes
RELEASE DATE 27 January 1933
PRODUCED BY Paramount Publix

## 9  Woman Accused ▽
DIRECTOR Paul Sloane
SCENARIO Bayard Veiller based on a story by
Polen Banks from a Liberty Magazine serial
multi-authored by Rupert Hughes, Vicki
Baum, Zane Grey, Vina Delmar, Irvin S.
Cobb, Gertrude Atherton, J. P. McEvoy,
Ursula Parott, Polen Banks and Sophie
Kerr
PHOTOGRAPHY Karl Struss
CAST Glenda O'Brien (Nancy Carroll);
Jeffrey Baxter (Cary Grant); Stephen
Bessemer (John Halliday); District
Attorney Clarke (Irving Pichel); Leo Young
(Louis Calhern); Martha (Norma
Mitchell); Little Maxie (Jack La Rue);
Inspector Swope (Frank Sheridan); Dr
Simpson (John Lodge); Captain of Boat
(William J. Kelly); Judge Osgood (Harry
Holman); Tony Graham (Jay Belasco);
Evelyn Craig (Gertrude Messinger); Cora
Mathews (Lora Andre); The Steward
(Donald Stuart); The Band Leader
(Gregory Golubeff); Cheer Leader (Robert
Quirk); Third Girl (Amo Ingraham);
Second Boy (Dennis Beaufort); Third Boy
(Gaylord Pendleton)
RUNNING TIME 73 minutes
RELEASE DATE 17 February 1933
PRODUCED BY Paramount Publix

## 10  The Eagle and the Hawk ▷
DIRECTOR Stuart Walker
ASSOCIATE DIRECTOR Mitchell Leisen
SCENARIO Bogart Rogers and Seton I. Miller
based on a story by John Monk Saunders
PHOTOGRAPHY Harry Fishbeck
CAST Jeremiah Young (Frederic March);
Henry Crocker (Cary Grant); Mike
Richards (Jack Oakie); The Beautiful Lady
(Carole Lombard); Major Dunham (Sir
Guy Standing); Hogan (Forrester Harvey);
John Stevens (Kenneth Howell); Kingsford
(Layland Hodgson); Lady Erskine (Virginia
Hammond); General (Crawford Kent);
Tommy (Douglas Scott); Major Kruppman
(Robert Manning); Fanny (Adrienne
D'Ambricourt); French General's Aide
(Jaques Jou-Jerville); Flight Sergeant
(Russell Scott); French General (Paul
Cremonesi); Taxi Driver (Yorke Sherwood)
RUNNING TIME 72 minutes
RELEASE DATE 19 May 1933
PRODUCED BY Paramount Publix

## 11  Gambling Ship △
DIRECTOR Louis Gasnier and Max Marcin
SCENARIO Max Marcin and Seton I. Miller;
adapted by Claude Binyon from stories by
Peter Ruric
PHOTOGRAPHY Charles Lang
CAST Ace Corbin (Cary Grant); Eleanor La
Velle (Benita Hume); Blooey (Roscoe
Karns); Jeanne Sands (Glenda Farrell);
Pete Manning (Jack La Rue); Joe Burke
(Arthur Vinton); Baby Face (Charles
Williams); District Attorney (Edwin
Maxwell); First Gunman (Harry Shutan);
Second Gunman (Frank Moran); First
Detective (Spencer Charles); Second
Detective (Otho Wright); Indian Woman
(Evelyn Silvie); Woman Detective (Kate
Campbell); First Deputy (Edward Gargan);
Second Deputy (Jack Grey); Conductor
(William Welsh); The Sailor (Sid Saylor);
Doctor (Hooper Atchley); Telephone
Operator (Larry Alexander); Croupier
(Louis Natheaux); Cook (Gum Chung)
RUNNING TIME 72 minutes
RELEASE DATE 23 June 1933
PRODUCED BY Paramount Publix

## 12  I'm No Angel ▽
DIRECTOR Wesley Ruggles
SCENARIO original screenplay and dialogue
by Mae West; continuity by Harlan
Thompson, with suggestions by Lowell
Brentano
PHOTOGRAPHY Leo Tover
CAST Tira (Mae West); Jack Clayton (Cary
Grant); Bill Barton (Edward Arnold); Slick
(Rolf Harolds); Barker (Russell Hopton);
Alicia Hatton (Gertrude Michael); Kirk
Lawrence (Kent Taylor); Thelma (Dorothy
Peterson); Benny Pinkowitz (Gregory
Ratoff); Beulah (Gertrude Howard); The
Chump (William Davidson); Rajah (Nigel
de Brulier); Bob, the Attorney (Irving
Pichel); Omnes (George Bruggeman);
Harry (Nat Pendleton); Chauffeur (Morrie
Cohen); Judge (Walter Walker)
RUNNING TIME 87 minutes
RELEASE DATE 6 October 1933
PRODUCED BY Paramount Publix

## 13  Alice in Wonderland
DIRECTOR Norman McLeod
SCENARIO Joseph L Mankiewicz and
William Cameron Menzies from original
material by Lewis Carroll
PHOTOGRAPHY Henry Sharp and Bert
Glennon
EDITOR Edward Hoagland
CAST Alice (Charlotte Henry); Cheshire Cat
(Richard Arlen); Fish (Roscoe Ates);
Gryphon (William Austine); White Knight
(Gary Cooper); Leg of Mutton (Jack
Duffy); Uncle Gilbert (Leon Errol); White
Queen (Louise Fazenda); Humpty Dumpty
(W. C. Fields); King of Hearts (Alec B.
Francis); White Rabbit (Skeets Gallagher);
Mock Turtle (Cary Grant); Cook (Lillian
Harmer); Mouse (Raymond Hatton); Frog
(Sterling Holloway); Mad Hatter (Edward
Everett Horton); Tweedledee (Roscoe
Karns); Joker (Baby LeRoy); Father
William's Son (Lucien Littlefield); Sheep
(Mae Marsh); Dodo Bird (Polly Moran);
Tweedledum (Jack Oakie); Red Queen
(Edna May Oliver); Plum Pudding (George
Ovey); Queen of Hearts (May Robson);
March Hare (Charlie Ruggles); Dormouse
(Jackie Searle); Duchess (Alison
Skipworth); Caterpillar (Ned Sparks)
RUNNING TIME 90 minutes
RELEASE DATE 22 December 1933
PRODUCED BY Paramount Publix

**14 Thirty-Day Princess** ▽
DIRECTOR Marion Gering
SCENARIO Preston Sturges and Frank
Partos; adaptation by Sam Hellman and
Edwin Justus Mayer from original story by
Clarence Buddington Kelland
PHOTOGRAPHY Leon Shamroy
CAST Princess Catterina (Sylvia Sidney);
Nancy Lane (Sylvia Sidney); Porter
Madison (Cary Grant); Richard Gresham
(Edward Arnold); King Anatole (Henry
Stephenson); Count Nicholaus (Vince
Barnett); The Baron (Edgar Norton); Mr
Kirk (Ray Walker); Parker (Lucien
Littlefield); Managing Editor (Robert
McWade); Spottswood (George Baxter);
Lady in Waiting (Marguerite Namara)
RUNNING TIME 73 minutes
RELEASE DATE 18 May 1934
PRODUCED BY B. P. Schulberg Productions

**15 Born to be Bad** △
DIRECTOR Lowell Sherman
SCENARIO Story, dialogue and adaptation by
Ralph Graves; continuity by Harrison
Jacobs
PHOTOGRAPHY Barney McGill
EDITOR Maurice Wright
CAST Letty Strong (Loretta Young); Mickey
(Jackie Kelk); Malcolm Trevor (Cary
Grant); Fuzzy (Henry Travers); Steve
Karns (Russell Hopton); Max Lieber
(Andrew Tombes); Doctor Dropsy
(Howard Lang); Adolph (Harry Green);
Alice Trevor (Marion Burns); Lawyer (Paul
Harvey); Butler (Charles Coleman); Truant

Officer (Matt Briggs); Miss Crawford
(Geneva Mitchell)
RUNNING TIME 61 minutes
RELEASE DATE 18 May 1934
PRODUCED BY Twentieth Century

**16 Kiss and Make Up** ▽
DIRECTOR Harlan Thompson
SCENARIO Harlan Thompson and George
Marion Jr.; original by Steve Beckeffi,
adapted by Jane Hinton
PHOTOGRAPHY Leon Shamroy
CAST Dr Maurice Lamar (Cary Grant);
Anne (Helen Mack); Eve Caron (Genevieve
Tobin); Marcel Caron (Edward Everett
Horton); Max Pascal (Lucien Littlefield);
Countess Rita (Mona Maris); Vilma
(Katherine Williams); Magda (Lucille
Lund); Rolando (Rafael Storm); Mme
Severac (Mme Bonita); Mme Durand
(Doris Lloyd); Maharajah of Baroona
(Milton Wallace); Plumber (Sam Ashe);
Landlady (Helena Phillips); Consuelo of
Claghorne (Toby Wing); Chairman of
banquet (Henry Armetta); Jean the valet
(George Andre Beranger); Beauty clinic
nurses (Judith Arlen, Jean Gale, Hazel
Hayes, Lee Ann Meredith); Radio
announcer (Helen Cohan); Maharajah's
wife (Jean Carmen); Radio listener (GiGi
Parrish); Lady Rummond-Dray (Anne
Hovey); Beauty clinic patients (Betty
Bryson and Jacqueline Wells and the
Wampas Baby Stars of 1934)
RUNNING TIME 80 minutes
RELEASE DATE 13 July 1934
PRODUCED BY B. P. Schulberg

**17 Ladies Should Listen**
DIRECTOR Frank Tuttle
SCENARIO Claude Binyon and Frank Butler;
original by Alfred Savoir and Guy Bolton
PHOTOGRAPHY Harry Sharp
CAST Julian de Lussac (Cary Grant); Anna
Mirelle (Frances Drake); Paul Vernet
(Edward Everett Horton); Marguerite
Cintos (Rosita Moreno); Joseph Flamberg
(George Barlier); Susie Flamberg (Nydia
Westman); Henri (Porter) (Charles Ray);
Albert (Manservant) (Charles Arnt);
Ramon Cintos (Rafael Corio); Blanche
(Operator) (Clara Lou Sheridan); Operator
(Henrietta Burnside); Butler (Joe North)

RUNNING TIME 62 minutes
RELEASE DATE 10 August 1934
PRODUCED BY Douglas MacLean

**18 Enter Madame!** ▽
DIRECTOR Elliot Nugent
SCENARIO Charles Brackett and Gladys
Lehman based on original play by Gilda
Varesi Archibald and Dorothea Donn-
Byrne
PHOTOGRAPHY Theodor Sparkuhl and
William Mellor
CAST Lisa Della Robbia (Elissa Landi);
Gerald Fitzgerald (Cary Grant); Mr
Farnum (Lynne Overman); Flora Preston
(Sharon Lynne); Bice (Michelette Burani);
Archimede (Paul Forcasi); The Doctor
(Adrian Rosley); Aline Chalmers (Cecelia
Parker); John Fitzgerald (Frank
Albertson); Tamamoto (Wilfred Hari);
Carlson (Torben Meyer); Bjorgenson
(Harold Berquist); Operator (Diana Lewis);
Scarpia (on stage) (Richard Bonelli)
RUNNING TIME 83 minutes
RELEASE DATE 4 January 1935
PRODUCED BY Paramount Publix

## 19 Wings in the Dark △
DIRECTOR James Flood
SCENARIO Jack Kirkland and Frank Partos;
adaptation by Dale Van Every and E. H.
Robinson; original by Nell Shipman and
Philip D. Hurn
PHOTOGRAPHY William C Mellor
CAST Sheila Mason (Myrna Loy); Ken
Gordon (Cary Grant); Nick Williams
(Roscoe Karns); Mac (Hobart
Cavanaugh); Tops Harmon (Dean Jagger);
Yipp Morgan (Bert Hanlon); Joy Burns
(James Burtis); Jake Brashear (Russell
Hopton); Kennel Club Secretary (Samuel S.
Hinds); The Doctor (Arnold Korff);
Sheila's first mechanic (Matt McHugh);
Radio announcer (Graham McNamee);
Cameraman (Alfred Delcambre)
RUNNING TIME 75 minutes
RELEASE DATE 1 February 1935
PRODUCED BY Paramount Pictures

CAST Michael Andrews (Cary Grant); John
Stevenson (Claude Rains); Rosemary
Haydon (Gertrude Michael); Ilya (Kathleen
Burke); Lieutenant Prescott (Colin Tapley);
Mirov (Akim Tamiroff); Corporal Foster
(Billy Bevan); Turkish major (Georges
Renevant); Nurse Rowland (Margaret
Swope); Cullen (Jameson Thomas); Haidor
(Nick Shaid); Amrak (Harry Semels);
Armenian patriarch (Meyer Ouhayoun);
Armenian officer (Frazier Acosta);
Armenian guard (Malay Clu); Head nurse
(Elspeth Dudgeon); Nurse (Beulah
McDonald); Sergeant in general's office
(Robert Adair); Sergeant Bates (William
Brown); General (Claude King); Doctor
(Olaf Hytten); Colonel (Frank Elliott);
Surgeon (Frank Dawson)
RUNNING TIME 75 minutes
RELEASE DATE 11 October 1935
PRODUCED BY Paramount Pictures

Jimmy Monkley (Cary Grant); Michael
Fane (Brian Aherne); Henry Scarlett
(Edmund Gwenn); Lily (Natalie Paley);
Maudie Tilt (Dennie Moore); Drunk
(Lennox Pawle)
RUNNING TIME 94 minutes
RELEASE DATE 3 January 1936
PRODUCED BY RKO Radio

## 22 Big Brown Eyes ▽
DIRECTOR Raoul Walsh
SCENARIO Raoul Walsh and Bert Hanlon;
original story by James Edward Grant
PHOTOGRAPHY George Clemens
EDITOR Robert Simpson
CAST Danny Barr (Cary Grant); Eve Fallon
(Joan Bennett); Richard Morey (Walter
Pidgeon); Russ Cortig (Lloyd Nolan); Cary
Butler (Alan Baxter); Mrs Cole (Marjorie
Gateson); Bessie Blair (Isabel Jewell);
Benny Bottle (Douglas Fowley); Don
Butler (Henry Kleinbach); Jack Sully
(Joseph Sawyer); Cashier (Dolores Casey);
Myrtle (Doris Canfield); Editor (Edwin
Maxwell); Mother (Helen Brown); Martin
(Sam Flint); Defense attorney (Joe Picorri);
Prosecuting attorney (Charlie Wilson); Red
(Charles Martin); Malley (Francis
McDonald); Joe (Eddie Conrad);
Chauffeur (Ed Jones)
RUNNING TIME 76 minutes
RELEASE DATE 3 April 1936
PRODUCED BY A. Walter Wanger

## 20 The Last Outpost △
DIRECTOR Charles Barton and Louis
Gasnier
SCENARIO Philip MacDonald; adaptation by
Frank Partos and Charles Brackett; story
by F. Britten Austin
PHOTOGRAPHY Theodor Sparkuhl
EDITOR Jack Dennis

## 21 Sylvia Scarlett △
DIRECTOR George Cukor
SCENARIO Gladys Unger, John Collier and
Mortimer Affner from the novel by
Compton Mackenzie
PHOTOGRAPHY Joseph August
EDITOR Jane Loring
CAST Sylvia Scarlett (Katherine Hepburn);

## 23 Suzy △
DIRECTOR George Fitzmaurice
SCENARIO Dorothy Parker, Alan Campbell,
Horace Jackson and Lenore Coffee from
novel by Herbert Gorman
PHOTOGRAPHY Ray June
EDITOR George Boemler
CAST Suzy (Jean Harlow); Terry (Franchot

179

Tone); Andre (Cary Grant); Baron (Lewis
Stone); Madame Eyrelle (Benita Hume);
Captain Barsanges (Reginald Mason);
Maisie (Inez Courtney); Mrs Schmidt
(Greta Meyer); 'Knobby' (David Clyde);
'Pop' Gaspard (Christian Rub); Gaston
(George Spelvin); Landlady (Una
O'Connor); Producer (Charles Judels);
Revue producer (Theodore Von Eltz);
Officer (Stanley Morner)
RUNNING TIME 95 minutes
RELEASE DATE 24 July 1936
PRODUCED BY Metro Goldwyn Mayer

## 24  Wedding Present △
DIRECTOR Richard Wallace
SCENARIO original story by Paul Gallico
PHOTOGRAPHY Leon Shamroy
EDITOR Robert Bischoff
CAST Rusty (Joan Bennett); Charlie (Cary
Grant); 'Stagg' (George Bancroft);
Dodacker (Conrad Nagel); Archduke
(Gene Lockhart); 'Smiles' Benson (William
Demarest); Mary Lawson (Inez Courtney);
Squinty (Edward Brophy); VanDorn
(Purnell Pratt); Willett (Douglas Wood);
Blaker (George Meeker); Laura Dodacker
(Lois Wilson); Jonathan (John Henry
Allen); Sammy Smith (George Offerman
Jr.); Haley (Damon Ford); German Band
(Heine Conklin, Billy Engel, Ray Hanson);
Six Reporters (Jack Mulhall, Cy Ring,
Charles Williams, Marshall Ruth, Eddie
Phillips, Allen Fox)
RUNNING TIME 81 minutes
RELEASE DATE 9 October 1936
PRODUCED BY Paramount Pictures

## 25  When You're in Love (GB title: For You Alone)  ▽
DIRECTOR Robert Riskin
SCENARIO Robert Riskin; story based on an
idea by Ethel Hill and Cedric Worth
PHOTOGRAPHY Joseph Walker
EDITOR Gene Milford
CAST Louise Fuller (Grace Moore); Jimmy
Hudson (Cary Grant); Marianne Woods
(Aline MacMahon); Walter Mitchell
(Henry Stephenson); Hank Miller (Thomas
Mitchell); Jane Summers (Catherine
Doucet); Luis Perugini (Luis Alberni);

Gerald Meeker (Gerald Oliver Smith); Mrs
Hamilton (Emma Dunn); Mr Hamilton
(George Pearce); Carlos (Frank Puglia)
RUNNING TIME 110 minutes
RELEASE DATE 27 February 1937
PRODUCED BY Columbia

## 26  The Amazing Quest of Ernest Bliss (GB title: Romance and Riches)  ▽
DIRECTOR Alfred Zeisler
SCENARIO John L. Balderston; from a story
by E. Phillips Oppenheim
PHOTOGRAPHY Otto Heller
CAST Ernest Bliss (Cary Grant); Frances
(Mary Brian); Sir James Aldroyd (Peter
Gawthorne); Lord Honiton (Henry
Kendall); Dorrington (Leon M Lion);
Masters (John Turnbull); Crawley (Arthur
Hardy); Clare (Iris Ashley); The Buyer
(Garry Marsh); Giuseppe (Andrea
Malandrinos); Montague (Alfred
Wellesley); Mrs Heath (Marie Wright); Mrs
Mott (Buena Bent); Scales (Charles
Farrell); Bill Bronson (Hal Gordon);
Clowes (Quinton MacPherson)
RUNNING TIME 70 minutes
RELEASE DATE 6 March 1937
PRODUCED BY Garrett Klement Pictures

## 27  Topper △
DIRECTOR Norman Z. McLeod
SCENARIO Jack Jerne, Eric Hatch and Eddie
Moran, from a story by Thorne Smith
PHOTOGRAPHY Norbert Brodine
CAST Marion Kerby (Constance Bennett);
George Kerby (Cary Grant); Cosmo
Topper (Roland Young); Mrs Topper (Billie
Burke); Wilkins (Alan Mowbray); Casey
(Eugene Pallette); Elevator Boy (Arthur
Lake); Mrs Stuyvesant (Hedda Hopper);
Miss Johnson (Virginia Sale); Hotel
manager (Theodore Von Eltz); Policeman
(J. Farrell McDonald); Secretary (Elaine
Shepard); 'Three Hits and a Miss'
(Themselves)
RUNNING TIME 98 minutes
RELEASE DATE 16 July 1937
PRODUCED BY Hal Roach

## 28  The Toast of New York  △
DIRECTOR Rowland V. Lee
SCENARIO Dudley Nichols, John Twist and
Joes Sayre, from Book of Daniel Drew by
Bouck White and Robber Barons by
Matthew Josephson
PHOTOGRAPHY Peverell Marley
EDITOR George Hively
CAST Jim Fisk (Edward Arnold); Nick

Boyd (Cary Grant); Josie Mansfield
(Frances Farmer); Luke (Jack Oakie);
Daniel Drew (Donald Meek); Fleurigue
(Thelma Leeds); Vanderbilt (Clarence
Kolb); Photographer (Billy Gilbert);
Broker (George Irving); Lawyers (Frank
M. Thomas, Russell Hicks); Wallack
(Oscar Apfel); President of the Board
(Lionel Belmore); Bellhop (Robert
McClung); Janitor (Robert Dudley); Beef
Dooley (Dewey Robinson); Top Sergeant
(Stanley Fields); Major (Gavin Gordon);
Mary Lou (Joyce Crompton); Virginia Lee
(Virginia Carroll)
RUNNING TIME 109 minutes
RELEASE DATE 30 July 1937
PRODUCED BY RKO Radio

## 29 The Awful Truth △
DIRECTOR Leo McCarey
SCENARIO Vina Delmar; story by Arthur
Richmond
PHOTOGRAPHY Joseph Walker
EDITOR Al Clark
CAST Lucy Warriner (Irene Dunne); Jerry
Warriner (Cary Grant); Daniel Leeson
(Ralph Bellamy); Armand Duvalle
(Alexander D'Arcy); Aunt Patsy (Cecil
Cunningham); Barbara Vance (Marguerite
Churchill); Mrs Leeson (Esther Dale);
Toots Binswanger (Dixie Belle Lee) (Joyce
Compton); Frank Randall (Robert Allen);
Mr Vance (Robert Warwick); Lord Fabian
(Claud Allister); Lady Fabian (Zita
Moulton)
RUNNING TIME 89 minutes
RELEASE DATE 21 October 1937
PRODUCED BY Columbia Pictures

## 30 Bringing Up Baby ▷
DIRECTOR Howard Hawks
SCENARIO Dudley Nichols and Hager Wilde;
from a story by Hager Wilde
PHOTOGRAPHY Russell Metty
EDITOR George Hively
CAST Susan (Katherine Hepburn); David
Huxley (Cary Grant); Major Horace
Applegate (Charles Ruggles); Slocum
(Walter Catlett); Mr Gogarty (Barry
Fitzgerald); Aunt Elizabeth (May Robson);
Dr Lehmann (Fritz Feld); Mrs Gogarty
(Leona Roberts); Mr Peabody (George
Irving); Mrs Lehmann (Tala Birrell); Alice
Swallow (Virginia Walker); Elmer (John
Kelly)
RUNNING TIME 102 minutes
RELEASE DATE 18 February 1938
PRODUCED BY RKO Radio

## 31 Holiday (GB titles: Free to Live, △ Unconventional Linda)
DIRECTOR George Cukor
SCENARIO Donald Ogden Stewart and
Sidney Buchman; original story by Philip
Barry
PHOTOGRAPHY Franz Planer
EDITORS Otto Meyer and Al Clark
CAST Linda Seton (Katherine Hepburn);
Johnny Case (Cary Grant); Julia Seton
(Doris Nolan); Ned Seton (Lew Ayres);
Nick Potter (Edward Everett Horton);
Edward Seton (Henry Kolker); Laura
Cram (Binnie Barnes); Susan Potter (Jean
Dixon); Seton Cram (Henry Daniell)
RUNNING TIME 94 minutes
RELEASE DATE 15 June 1938
PRODUCED BY Everett Riskin

## 32 Gunga Din ▷
DIRECTOR George Stevens
SCENARIO Joel Sayre and Fred Guiol; story
by Ben Hecht and Charles MacArthur,
inspired by Rudyard Kipling's poem *Gunga
Din*
PHOTOGRAPHY John H. August

EDITORS Henry Berman and John Lockert
CAST Cutter (Cary Grant); MacChesney
(Victor McLaglen); Ballantine (Douglas
Fairbanks Jr.); Gunga Din (Sam Jaffe);
Guru (Eduardo Ciannelli); Emmy (Joan
Fontaine); Colonel Weed (Montague
Love); Higginbotham (Robert Coote);
Chota (Abner Biberman); Major Mitchell
(Lumsden Hare)
RUNNING TIME 117 minutes
RELEASE DATE 17 February 1939
PRODUCED BY RKO Radio

## 33 Only Angels Have Wings △
DIRECTOR Howard Hawks
SCENARIO From a story by Howard Hawks
PHOTOGRAPHY Joseph Walker
EDITOR Viola Lawrence
CAST Jeff Carter (Cary Grant); Bonnie Lee
(Jean Arthur); Bat McPherson (Richard
Barthelmess); Judith (Rita Hayworth); Kid
Dabb (Thomas Mitchell); Dutchman (Sig
Ruman); Sparks (Victor Kilian); Gent
Shelton (John Carrol); Les Peters (Allyn
Joslyn); Tex Gordon (Donald Barry); Joe
Souther (Noah Beery Jr.); Lily (Melissa
Sierra); Dr Lagorio (Lucio Villegas);
Hartwood (Forbes Murray); The Singer
(Maciste); Mike (Pat Flaherty); Pancho
(Pedro Regas); Baldy (Pat West)
RUNNING TIME 121 minutes
RELEASE DATE 25 May 1939
PRODUCED BY Columbia

## 34 In Name Only ▽
DIRECTOR John Cromwell
SCENARIO Richard Sherman from novel
*Memory of Love* by Bessie Brewer
PHOTOGRAPHY J. Roy Hunt
EDITOR William Hamilton
CAST Julie Eden (Carole Lombard); Alec
Walker (Cary Grant); Maida Walker (Kay
Francis); Mr Walker (Charles Coburn);
Suzanne (Helen Vinson); Laura (Katharine
Alexander); Dr Gateson (Jonathan Hale);
Dr Muller (Maurice Moscovich); Mrs
Walker (Nella Walker); Ellen (Peggy Ann
Garner); Gardner (Spencer Charters)
RUNNING TIME 94 minutes
RELEASE DATE 18 August 1939
PRODUCED BY RKO Radio

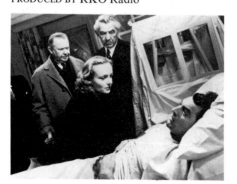

## 35 His Girl Friday △
DIRECTOR Howard Hawks
SCENARIO Charles Ledere, from the play *The
Front Page* by Ben Hecht and Charles
MacArthur
PHOTOGRAPHY Joseph Walker
EDITOR Gene Havlick
CAST Walter Burns (Cary Grant); Hildy
Johnson (Rosalind Russell); Bruce Baldwin
(Ralph Bellamy); Sheriff Hartwell (Gene
Lockhart); Murphy (Porter Hall); Bensiger
(Ernest Truex); Endicott (Cliff Edwards);
Mayor (Clarence Kolb); McCue (Roscoe
Karns); Wilson (Frank Jenks); Sanders
(Regis Toomey); Diamond Louie (Abner
Biberman); Duffy (Frank Orth); Earl
Williams (John Qualen); Mollie Malloy
(Helen Mack); Mrs Baldwin (Alma
Kruger); Silas F. Pinkus (Billy Gilbert);
Warden Cooley (Pat West); Dr Egelhoffer
(Edwin Maxwell)
RUNNING TIME 92 minutes
RELEASE DATE 18 January 1940
PRODUCED BY Columbia

## 36 My Favorite Wife △
DIRECTOR Garson Kanin
SCENARIO Story by Bella and Samuel
Spewack and Leo McCarey
PHOTOGRAPHY Rudolph Mate
EDITOR Robert Wise
CAST Ellen (Irene Dunne); Nick (Cary
Grant); Burkett (Randolph Scott); Bianca
(Gail Patrick); Ma (Ann Schoemaker); Tim
(Scotty Beckett); Chinch (Mary Lou
Harrington); Hotel Clerk (Donald
MacBride); Johnson (Hugh O'Connell);

Judge (Granville Bates); Dr Kohlmar
(Pedro de Cordoba)
RUNNING TIME 88 minutes
RELEASE DATE 17 May 1940
PRODUCED BY RKO Radio

## 37 The Howards of Virginia (GB title: The Tree of Liberty) ▽
DIRECTOR Frank Lloyd
SCENARIO Sidney Buchman, from the novel
*The Tree of Liberty* by Elizabeth Page
PHOTOGRAPHY Bert Glennon
EDITOR Paul Weatherwax
CAST Matt Howard (Cary Grant); Jan
Petyon-Howard (Martha Scott); Fleetwood
Peyton (Sir Cedric Hardwicke); Roger
Peyton (Alan Marshal); Thomas Jefferson
(Richard Carlson); Captain Jabez Allen
(Paul Kelly); Tom Norton (Irving Bacon);
Aunt Clarissa (Elizabeth Risdon); Mrs
Norton (Ann Revere); James Howard at 16
(Richard Alden); Peyton Howard at 18
(Phil Taylor); Mary Howard at 17 (Rita
Quigley); Dicey (Libby Taylor); Patrick
Henry (Richard Gaines); George
Washington (George Houston)
RUNNING TIME 117 minutes
RELEASE DATE 19 September 1940
PRODUCED BY Columbia

**38 The Philadelphia Story** △
DIRECTOR George Cukor
SCENARIO Donald Ogden Stewart; based on play by Philip Barry as produced by Theatre Guild Inc.
PHOTOGRAPHY Joseph Ruttenberg
EDITOR Frank Sullivan
CAST C. K. Dexter Haven (Cary Grant); Tracy Lord (Katherine Hepburn); Macauley Connor (James Stewart); Elizabeth Imbrie (Ruth Hussey); George Kittredge (John Howard); Uncle Willie (Roland Young); Seth Lord (John Halliday); Margaret Lord (Mary Nash); Dinah Lord (Virginia Weidler); Sidney Kidd (Henry Daniell); Edward (Lionel Pape)
RUNNING TIME 112 minutes
RELEASE DATE 17 January 1941
PRODUCED BY Metro-Goldwyn-Mayer

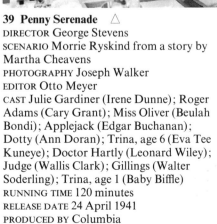

**39 Penny Serenade** △
DIRECTOR George Stevens
SCENARIO Morrie Ryskind from a story by Martha Cheavens
PHOTOGRAPHY Joseph Walker
EDITOR Otto Meyer
CAST Julie Gardiner (Irene Dunne); Roger Adams (Cary Grant); Miss Oliver (Beulah Bondi); Applejack (Edgar Buchanan); Dotty (Ann Doran); Trina, age 6 (Eva Tee Kuneye); Doctor Hartly (Leonard Wiley); Judge (Wallis Clark); Gillings (Walter Soderling); Trina, age 1 (Baby Biffle)
RUNNING TIME 120 minutes
RELEASE DATE 24 April 1941
PRODUCED BY Columbia

**40 Suspicion** △
DIRECTOR Alfred Hitchcock
SCENARIO Samson Raphaelson, Joan Harrison and Alma Reville, from *Before the Fact* by Francis Iles
PHOTOGRAPHY Harry Stradling
EDITOR William Hamilton
CAST Johnnie (Cary Grant); Lina McLaidlaw (Joan Fontaine); General McLaidlaw (Sir Cedric Hardwicke); Beaky (Nigel Bruce); Mrs McLaidlaw (Dame May Whitty); Mrs Newsham (Isabel Jeans); Ethel the maid (Heather Angel); Isobel Sedbusk (Auriol Lee); Reggie Wetherby (Reginald Sheffield); Captain Melbeck (Leo G. Carroll)
RUNNING TIME 99 minutes
RELEASE DATE 14 November 1941
PRODUCED BY RKO Radio

**41 The Talk of the Town** ▽
DIRECTOR George Stevens
SCENARIO Irwin Shaw and Sidney Buchman, adapted by Dale Van Every from an original story by Sidney Harmon
PHOTOGRAPHY Ted Tetzlaff
EDITOR Otto Meyer
CAST Leopold Dilg (Cary Grant); Nora Shelley (Jean Arthur); Michael Lightcap (Ronald Colman); Sam Yates (Edgar Buchanan); Regina Bush (Glenda Farrell); Andrew Holmes (Charles Dingle); Mrs Shelley (Emma Dunn); Tilney (Rex Ingram); Jan Pulaski (Leonid Kinskey);

Clyde Bracken (Tom Tyler); Chief of Police (Don Beddoe); Judge Grnstadt (George Watts); Senator James Boyd (Clyde Fillmore); District Attorney (Frank M. Thomas); Forrester (Lloyd Bridges)
RUNNING TIME 118 minutes
RELEASE DATE 20 August 1942
PRODUCED BY Columbia

**42 Once Upon a Honeymoon** ▽
DIRECTOR Leo McCarey
SCENARIO Sheridan Gibney; original story by Leo McCarey
PHOTOGRAPHY George Barnes
EDITOR Theron Warth
CAST Katie (Ginger Rogers); Pat O'Toole (Cary Grant); Baron Von Luber (Walter Slezak); Le Blanc (Albert Dekker); Borelski (Albert Bassermann); Elsa (Ferike Boros); Cumberland (Harry Shannon); Anna (Natasha Lytess); Dieinock (John Banner)
RUNNING TIME 116 minutes
RELEASE DATE 27 November 1942
PRODUCED BY RKO Radio

## 43 Mr Lucky △

DIRECTOR H. C. Potter
SCENARIO Milton Holmes and Adrian Scott, from *Bundles for Freedom* by Milton Holmes
PHOTOGRAPHY George Barnes
EDITOR Theron Warth
CAST Joe Adams (Cary Grant); Dorothy Bryant (Laraine Day); Hard Swede (Charles Bickford); Captain Steadman (Gladys Cooper); Crunk (Alan Carney); Mr Bryant (Henry Stephenson); Zepp (Paul Stewart); Mrs Ostrander (Kay Johnson); Greek Priest (Vladimir Sokoloff); Commissioner Hargreaves (Walter Kingsford); Gaffer (Erford Gage); McDougal (J. M. Kerrigan); Foster (Edward Fielding); Siga (John Bleifer); Joe Bascopolus (Juan Varro); Dealer (Don Brodie)
RUNNING TIME 100 minutes
RELEASE DATE 1943
PRODUCED BY RKO Radio

## 44 Destination Tokyo △

DIRECTOR Delmer Daves
SCENARIO Delmer Daves and Albert Maltz, from an original story by Steve Fisher
PHOTOGRAPHY Bert Glennon
EDITOR Chris Nyby
CAST Captain Cassidy (Cary Grant); Wolf (John Garfield); Cookie (Alan Hale); Reserve (John Ridgely); Tin Can (Dane Clark); Executive (Warner Anderson); Pills (William Prince); Tommy (Robert Hutton); Dakota (Peter Whitney); Mike (Tom Tully); Mrs Cassidy (Faye Emerson); English Officer (Warren Douglas); Sparks (John Forsythe); Sound Man (John Alvin); Torpedo Officer (Bill Kennedy); Quartermaster (William Challee); Yo Yo (Whit Bissell); Commanding Officer (John Whitney); Chief of Boat (George Lloyd); Toscanini (Maurice Murphy)
RUNNING TIME 135 minutes
RELEASE DATE 1 January 1944
PRODUCED BY Warner Brothers

## 45 Once Upon a Time △

DIRECTOR Alexander Hall
SCENARIO Lewis Meltzer and Oscar Saul; adapted by Irving Fineman. Based on a radio play *My Client Curly* by Norman Corwin and Lucille F. Herrmann
PHOTOGRAPHY Franz F. Planer
EDITOR Gene Havlick
CAST Jerry Flynn (Cary Grant); Jeannie Thompson (Janet Blair); 'The Moke' (James Gleason); Pinky Thompson (Ted Donaldson); McKenzie (Howard Freeman); Brandt (William Demarest); Gabriel Heatter (Art Baker); Dunhill (Paul Stanton); Fatso (Mickey McGuire)
RUNNING TIME 89 minutes
RELEASE DATE 11 May 1944
PRODUCED BY Columbia

## 46 None But the Lonely Heart ▷

DIRECTOR Clifford Odets
SCENARIO Clifford Odets from novel by Richard Llewellyn
PHOTOGRAPHY George Barnes
EDITOR Rolan Gross
CAST Ernie Mott (Cary Grant); His mother, Ma Mott (Ethel Barrymore); Aggie Hunter (Jane Wyatt); Ada (June Duprez); Twite (Barry Fitzgerald); Jim Mordinoy (George Coulouris); Did Pettyjohn (Roman Bohnen); Ike Weber, pawnbroker (Konstantin Shayne); Lew Tate (Dan Duryea); Mrs Tate (Rosalind Ivan); Miss Tate (Dierdre Vale); Ma Chalmers (Eva Leonard Boyne); Ma Snowden (Queenie Vassar); Millie Wilson (Katherine Allen); Cash (Joseph Vitale); Taz (Morton Lowry); Knocker (William Challee); Slush (Skelton Knagg); Ma Segiviss (Virginia Farmer); Marjoriebanks (Art Smith); Ike Lesser (Milton Wallace); Sister Nurse (Helen Thimig); Flo (Renie Riano); Percy (Marcel Dill)
RUNNING TIME 113 minutes
RELEASE DATE 22 September 1944
PRODUCED BY RKO Radio

## 47 Arsenic and Old Lace △
DIRECTOR Frank Capra
SCENARIO Julius J. Epstein and Philip G.
Epstein from the play by Joseph Kesselring
PHOTOGRAPHY Sol Polito
EDITOR Daniel Mandell
CAST Mortimer Brewster (Cary Grant);
Jonathan Brewster (Raymond Massey);
Elaine Harper (Priscilla Lane); Abby
Brewster (Josephine Hull); Martha
Brewster (Jean Adair); O'Hara (Jack
Carson); Mr Witherspoon (Edward Everett
Horton); Dr Einstein (Peter Lorre);
Lieutenant Rooney (James Gleason);
Teddy 'Roosevelt' Brewster (John
Alexander); Reverend Harper (Grant
Mitchell); Braphy (Edward McNamara);
Taxi Driver (Garry Owen); Saunders (John
Ridgely); Judge Cullman (Vaughan
Glaser); Doctor Gilchrist (Chester Clute);
Reporter (Charles Lane); Gibbs (Edward
McWade); Man in Phone Booth (Leo
White); Marriage License Clerk (Spencer
Charters); Photographer (Hank Mann);
Umpire (Lee Phelps)
RUNNING TIME 118 minutes
RELEASE DATE 23 September 1944
PRODUCED BY Warner Bros.

## 48 Night and Day △
DIRECTOR Michael Curtiz
SCENARIO Charles Hoffman, Leo Townsend
and William Bowers; based on the career of
Cole Porter
PHOTOGRAPHY Peverell Marley and William
Skall
EDITOR David Weisbart
CAST Cole Porter (Cary Grant); Linda Lee
Porter (Alexis Smith); Himself (Monty
Woolley); Carol Hill (Ginny Simms);

Gracie Harris (Jane Wyman); Gabrielle
(Eve Arden); Anatole Giron (Victor
Francen); Leon Dowling (Alan Hale);
Nancy (Dorothy Malone); Bernie (Tom
D'Andrea); Kate Porter (Selena Royle);
Ward Blackburn (Donald Woods); Omar
Porter (Henry Stephenson) Bart
McClelland (Paul Cavanagh); Wilowsky
(Sig Ruman); Specialty Singer (Carlos
Ramirez); Specialty Dancer (Milda
Mladova); Specialty Dancer (George
Zoritch); Specialty Team (Adam and Jayne
DiGatano); Caleb (Clarence Muse); Petsy
(John Alvin); O'Hallaran (George Riley);
Producer (Howard Freeman); Director
(Bobby Watson); First Peaches (John
Pearson); Second Peaches (Herman Bing);
Herself (Mary Martin)
RUNNING TIME 132 minutes
RELEASE DATE 2 July 1946
PRODUCED BY Warner Bros

## 49 Notorious △
DIRECTOR Alfred Hitchcock
SCENARIO Ben Hecht from an original
subject by Alfred Hitchcock
PHOTOGRAPHY Ted Tetzlaff
EDITOR Theron Warth
CAST Devlin (Cary Grant); Alicia
Huberman (Ingrid Bergman); Alexander
Sebastian (Claude Rains); Paul Prescott
(Louis Calhern); Mme Sebastian (Madame
Konstantin); 'Dr Anderson' (Reinhold
Schunzel); Walter Beardsley (Moroni
Olsen); Eric Mathis (Ivan Triesault);
Joseph (Alex Minotis); Mr Hopkins (Wally
Brown); Ernest Weylin (Gavin Gordon);
Commodore (Sir Charles Mendl); Dr
Barbosa (Ricardo Costa); Hupka
(Eberhard Krumschmidt); Ethel (Fay
Baker)
RUNNING TIME 103 minutes
RELEASE DATE 22 July 1946
PRODUCED BY RKO Radio

## 50 The Bachelor and the Bobby Soxer (GB title: Bachelor Knight) ▽
DIRECTOR Irving Reis
SCENARIO original story and screenplay by
Sidney Sheldon
PHOTOGRAPHY Robert de Grasse, Nicholas
Musuraca
EDITOR Frederic Knudtson
CAST Dick (Cary Grant); Margaret (Myrna
Loy); Susan (Shirley Temple); Tommy
(Rudy Vallee); Beemesh (Ray Collins);

Thaddeua (Harry Davenport); Jerry
(Johnny Sands); Tony (Don Beddoe);
Bessie (Lillian Randolph); Agnes Prescott
(Veda Ann Borg); Walters (Dan Tobin);
Judge Treadwell (Ransom Sherman);
Winters (William Bakewell); Melvin (Irving
Bacon); Perry (Ian Bernard); Florence
(Carol Hughes); Anthony Herman (William
Hall); Maitre d'Hotel (Gregory Gay)
RUNNING TIME 95 minutes
RELEASE DATE 1 September 1947
PRODUCED BY Dore Schary Productions

## 51 The Bishop's Wife ▽
DIRECTOR Henry Koster
SCENARIO Robert Sherwood and Leonard
Bercorici from a novel by Robert Nathan
PHOTOGRAPHY Gregg Toland
EDITOR Monica Collingwood
CAST Dudley (Cary Grant); Julia Brougham
(Loretta Young); Henry Brougham (David
Niven); Professor Wutheridge (Monty
Wooley); Sylvester (James Gleason); Mrs
Hamilton (Gladys Cooper); Matilda (Elsa
Lanchester); Mildred Cassaway (Sara
Haden); Debby Brougham (Karolyn
Grimes); Maggenti (Tito Vuolo); Mr Miller
(Regis Toomey); Mrs Duffy (Sara
Edwards); Miss Trumbull (Margaret

McWade); Mrs Ward (Ann O'Neal); Mr
Perry (Ben Erway); Stevens (Erville
Alderson); Defense Captain (Bobby
Anderson); Attack Captain (Teddy Infuhr);
Michel (Eugene Borden); First Lady in
Michel's (Almira Sessions); Second Lady
(Claire DuBrey); Third Lady (Florence
Auer); Hat Shop Proprietress (Margaret
Wells); Hat Shop Customer (Kitty O'Neill)
RUNNING TIME 105 minutes
RELEASE DATE 13 November 1947
PRODUCED BY Samuel Goldwyn Productions

### 52  Mr Blandings Builds his Dream House
DIRECTOR H. C. Potter
SCENARIO Norman Panama and Melvin
Frank, based on a novel by Eric Hodgins
PHOTOGRAPHY James Wong Howe
EDITOR Harry Marker
CAST Jim Blandings (Cary Grant); Muriel
Blandings (Myrna Loy); Bill Cole (Melvyn
Douglas); Simms (Reginald Denny); Joan
Blandings (Sharyn Moffett); Betsy
Blandings (Connie Marshall); Gussie
(Louise Beavers); Smith (Ian Wolfe);
Tesander (Harry Shannon); Mr Zucca (Tito
Vuolo); Joe Appollonion (Nestor Paiva);
John Retch (Jason Robards); Mary (Lurene
Tuttle); Carpenter Foreman (Lex Barker);
Mr P. Delford (Emory Parnell)
RUNNING TIME 94 minutes
RELEASE DATE 25 March 1948
PRODUCED BY RKO Radio

### 53  Every Girl Should be Married   △
DIRECTOR Don Hartman
SCENARIO Stephen Morehouse, Avery and
Don Hartman from a short story by
Eleanor Harris
PHOTOGRAPHY George E. Diskant
EDITOR Harry Marker
CAST Dr Madison Brown (Cary Grant);

Roger Sanford (Franchot Tone); Julie
Hudson (Diana Lynn); Anabel Sims (Betsy
Drake); Mr Spitzer (Alan Mowbray); Mary
Nolan (Elizabeth Risdon); San McNutt
(Richard Gaines); Gogarty (Harry
Hayden); Soda Clerk (Chick Chandler);
Violinist (Leon Belasco); Pierre (Fred
Essler); Saleslady (Anna Q. Nilsson)
RUNNING TIME 84 minutes
RELEASE DATE 25 December 1948
PRODUCED BY Don Hartman

### 54  I Was a Male War Bride (GB title: You Can't Sleep Here)   △
DIRECTOR Howard Hawks
SCENARIO Charles Lederer, Leonard
Spigelgass and Hagar Wilde from a novel
by Henri Rochard
PHOTOGRAPHY Norbert Brodine and O. H.
Borradaile
EDITOR James B. Clark
CAST Captain Henri Rochard (Cary Grant);
Lt Catherine Gates (Ann Sheridan);
Captain Jack Rumsey (William Neff); Tony
Jowitt (Eugene Gericke); WACs (Marion
Marshall, Randy Stewart); Innkeeper's
Assistant (Ruben Wendorf); Waiter (Lester
Sharpe); Seaman (Ken Tobey); Lieutenant
(Robert Stevenson); Bartender (Alfred
Linder); Chaplain (David McMahon);
Shore Patrol (Joe Haworth); Trumble (John
Whitney); Sergeants (William Pullen,
William Self); Shore Patrol (John Zilly);
Sergeant (Bill Murphy)
RUNNING TIME 105 minutes
RELEASE DATE 2 September 1949
PRODUCED BY Sol C. Siegel

### 55  Crisis   ▽
DIRECTOR Richard Brooks
SCENARIO Richard Brooks from the short
story The Doubters by George Tabori
PHOTOGRAPHY Ray June
EDITOR Robert J. Kern
CAST Dr Eugene Ferguson (Cary Grant);
Raoul Farrago (Jose Ferrer); Helen
Ferguson (Paula Raymond); Senora Isabel
Farrago (Signe Hasso); Col Adragon
(Ramon Navarro); Gonzales (Gilbert

Roland); Sam Proctor (Leon Ames); Dr
Emilio Nierra (Antonio Moreno); Rosa
Aldana (Teresa Celli); General Valdini
(Mario Siletti); Cariago (Vincente Gomez);
Senor Magano (Martin Garralaga); Father
Del Puento (Pedro de Cordoba); Senora
Farrago (Soledad Jimenez); Rubio (Jose
Dominguez); Marco Aldana (Robert
Tafur); Luis (Maurice Jara)
RUNNING TIME 95 minutes
RELEASE DATE 4 July 1950
PRODUCED BY Loew's Incorporated

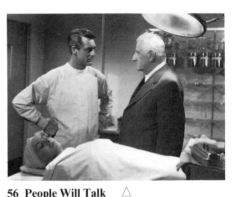

### 56  People Will Talk   △
DIRECTOR Joseph L. Mankiewicz
SCENARIO Joseph L. Mankiewicz; based on
the play Dr Praetorius by Curt Goetz
PHOTOGRAPHY Milton Krasner
EDITOR Barbara McLean
CAST Dr Noah Praetorius (Cary Grant);
Annabel Higgins (Jeanne Crain);
Shunderson (Findlay Currie); Prof. Elwell
(Hume Cronyn); Prof. Barker (Walter
Slezak); Arthur Higgins (Sidney Balckmer);
Dean Lyman Brockwell (Basil Ruysdael);
Miss James (Katherine Locke); John
Higgins (Will Wright); Miss Pickett
(Margaret Hamilton); Mrs Pegwhistle
(Esther Somers); Technician (Carleton
Young); Business Manager (Larry
Dobkin); Nurse (Jo Gilbert); Dietician
(Ann Morrison); Old Lady (Julia Dean);
Secretary (Gail Bonney); Student Manager
(William Klein); Haskins (George
Offerman); Mabel (Adele Longmire);
Coonan (Billy House); Photographer (Al
Murphy); Toy Salesman (Parley Baer);
Cook (Irene Seidner); Gussie (Joyce
MacKenzie); Night Matron (Maude
Wallack); Bella (Kay Lavelle); Doctor (Ray
Montgomery); Students (Paul Lees,
William Mauch, Leon Taylor)
RUNNING TIME 109 minutes
RELEASE DATE 2 September 1951
PRODUCED BY Darryl F. Zanuck

## 57 Room for One More △
DIRECTOR Norman Taurog
SCENARIO Jack Rose and Melville Shavelson from a book by Anna Perrott Rose
PHOTOGRAPHY Robert Burks
EDITOR Alan Crosland Jr
CAST 'Poppy' Rose (Cary Grant); Anna Rose (Betsy Drake); Miss Kenyon (Lurene Tuttle); Mrs Foreman (Randy Stuart); Harry Foreman (John Ridgely); The Mayor (Irving Bacon); Mrs Roberts (Mary Lou Treen); The Doctor (Hayden Rorke); Jane (Iris Mann); Teensie (George Winslow); Jimmy-John (Clifford Tatum Jr); Trot (Gay Gordon); Tim (Malcolm Cassell); Ben (Larry Olson)
RUNNING TIME 97 minutes
RELEASE DATE 26 January 1952
PRODUCED BY Henry Blanke

## 58 Monkey Business ▷
DIRECTOR Howard Hawks
SCENARIO Ben Hecht, I. A. L. Diamond and Charles Lederer from an unpublished story by Harry Segall
PHOTOGRAPHY Milton Krasner
EDITOR William B. Murphy
CAST Professor Barnaby Fulton (Cary Grant); Edwina Fulton (Ginger Rogers); Mr Oliver Oxley (Charles Coburn); Lois Laurel (Marilyn Monroe); Hank Entwhistle (Hugh Marlowe); Dr Siegfried Kitzel (Henri Letondal); Dr Zoldeck (Robert Cornthwaite); Mr G. J. Culverly (Larry Keating); Dr Bruner (Douglas Spencer); Mrs Rhinelander (Esther Dale); Little Indian (George Winslow)
RUNNING TIME 97 minutes
RELEASE DATE 15 September 1952
PRODUCED BY Sol C. Siegel

## 59 Dream Wife ▷
DIRECTOR Sidney Sheldon
SCENARIO Sidney Sheldon, Herbert Baker and Alfred L. Levitt; based on an

unpublished story by Alfred Lewis Levitt
PHOTOGRAPHY Milton Krasner
EDITOR George White
CAST Clemson Reade (Cary Grant); Effie (Deborah Kerr); Walter McBride (Walter Pidgeon); Tarji (Betta St John); Kahn (Eduard Franz); Vizier (Buddy Baer); Ken Landwell (Les Tremayne); Ali (Donald Randolph); Charlie Elkwood (Bruce Bennett); Henry Malvine (Richard Anderson); Mr Brown (Dan Tobin); Rima (Movita); Mrs Landwell (Gloria Holden); Mrs Elkwood (June Clayworth); George (Dean Miller); Louis (Steve Forrest); Sailor (Jonathan Cott); Pat (Patricia Tiernan)
RUNNING TIME 98 minutes
RELEASE DATE 19 June 1953
PRODUCED BY Loew's Incorporated

## 60 To Catch a Thief ▽
DIRECTOR Alfred Hitchcock
SCENARIO John Michael Hayes from a novel by David Dodge
PHOTOGRAPHY Robert Burks
EDITOR George Tomasini
CAST John Robie (Cary Grant); Frances Stevens (Grace Kelly); Mrs Stevens (Jessie Royce Landis); H. H. Hughson (John Williams); Bertani (Charles Vanel); Danielle (Brigitte Auber); Foussard (Jean Martinelli); Germaine (Georgette Anys)
RUNNING TIME 103 minutes
RELEASE DATE September 1955
PRODUCED BY Paramount Pictures

**61 The Pride and the Passion** △
DIRECTOR Stanley Kramer
SCENARIO Edna and Edward Anhalt; based on the novel *The Gun* by C. S. Forrester
PHOTOGRAPHY Franz Planer
EDITOR Frederic Knudtson & Ellsworth Hoagland
CAST Anthony (Cary Grant); Miguel (Frank Sinatra); Juana (Sophia Loren); General Jouvet (Theodore Bikel); Sermaine (John Wengraf); Ballinger (Jay Novello); Carlos (Jose Nieto); Vidal (Philip VanZandt); Jose (Carlos Larranaga); Manolo (Paco El Laberinto); Enrique (Julian Ugarte); Bishop (Felix De Pomes); Leonardo (Carlos Casaravilla); Ramon (Juan Olaguivel); Maria (Nana De Herrera); Francisco (Carlos De Mendoza); French Soldier (Luis Guedes)
RUNNING TIME 130 minutes
RELEASE DATE 10 July 1957
PRODUCED BY Stanley Kramer Pictures

**62 An Affair to Remember** ▽
DIRECTOR Leo McCarey
SCENARIO Delmer Daves and Leo McCarey; based on an unpublished original story by Leo McCarey and Mildred Cram
PHOTOGRAPHY Milton Krasner
EDITOR James B. Clark
CAST Nickie Ferrante (Cary Grant); Terry McKay (Deborah Kerr); Kenneth (Richard Denning); Lois Clarke (Neva Patterson);

Grandmother (Cathleen Nesbitt); Announcer (Robert Q. Lewis); Hathaway (Charles Watts); Courbet (Fortunio Bonanova); Father McGrath (Matt Moore); Miss Webb (Geraldine Wall); Miss Lane (Sarah Selby); Bartender (Alberto Morin); Gabrielle (Genevieve Aumont); Landlady (Jesslyn Fax); Gladys (Nora Marlowe)
RUNNING TIME 114 minutes
RELEASE DATE 2 July 1957
PRODUCED BY Jerry Wald Productions

**63 Kiss Them for Me** ▽
DIRECTOR Stanley Donen
SCENARIO Julius Epstein from the play *Kiss Them For Me* by Luther Davis and the novel *Shore Leave* by Frederic Wakeman
PHOTOGRAPHY Milton Krasner
EDITOR Robert Simpson
CAST Crewson (Cary Grant); Alice (Jayne Mansfield); Gwenneth (Suzy Parker); Eddie Turnbill (Leif Erikson); Mac, Lieutenant McCann (Ray Walston); Mississip (Larry Blyden); C. P. O. Ruddle (Nathaniel Frey); Commander Wallace (Werner Klemperer); Ensign Lewis (Jack Mullaney); RAF Pilot (Ben Wright); Gunner (Michael Ross); Roundtree (Harry Carey Jr.); Neilson (Frank Nelson); Debbie (Caprice Yordan); Lucille (Ann McCrea)
RUNNING TIME 103 minutes
RELEASE DATE 10 December 1957
PRODUCED BY Jerry Wald

**64 Indiscreet** △
DIRECTOR Stanley Donen
SCENARIO Norman Krasna, from his play *Kind Sir*
PHOTOGRAPHY Frederick A. Young
EDITOR Jack Harris
CAST Philip Adams (Cary Grant); Anna Kalman (Ingrid Bergman); Alfred Munson (Cecil Parker); Margaret Munson (Phyllis Calvert); Carl Banks (David Kossoff); Doris Banks (Megs Jenkins); Finleigh (Oliver Johnston); Finleigh's Clerk (Middleton Woods)
RUNNING TIME 100 minutes
RELEASE DATE 20 May 1958
PRODUCED BY Grandon Productions

**65 Houseboat** △
DIRECTOR Melville Shavelson
SCENARIO Melville Shavelson and Jack Rose
PHOTOGRAPHY Ray June
EDITOR Frank Fracht
CAST Tom Winston (Cary Grant); Cinzia Zaccardi (Sophia Loren); Caroline Gibson (Martha Hyer); Angelo (Harry Guardino); Arturo Zaccardi (Eduardo Ciannelli); Alan Wilson (Murray Hamilton); Elizabeth Winston (Mimi Gibson); David Winston (Paul Peterson); Robert Winston (Charles Herbert); Mrs Farnsworth (Madge Kennedy); Mr Farnsworth (John Litel); Harold Messner (Werner Klemperer)
RUNNING TIME 112 minutes
RELEASE DATE 19 November 1958
PRODUCED BY Jack Rose

**66 North by Northwest** ▽
DIRECTOR Alfred Hitchcock
SCENARIO Ernest Lehman
PHOTOGRAPHY Robert Burks
EDITOR George Tomasini
CAST Roger Thornhill (Cary Grant); Eve Kendall (Eva Marie Saint); Philip Vandamm (James Mason); Clara Thornhill (Jessie Royce Landis); Professor (Leo G. Carrol); Lester Townsend (Philip Ober); Handsome Woman (Josephine Hutchinson); Leonard (Martin Landau); Valerain (Adam Williams); Victor Larrabee (Edward Platt); Licht (Robert Ellenstein); Auctioneer (Les Tremayne); Dr Cross (Philip Coolidge); Chicago Policeman (Patrick McVey); Capt Junket (Edward Binns); Chicago Policeman (Ken Lynch)
RUNNING TIME 136 minutes
RELEASE DATE 17 July 1959
PRODUCED BY Loew's Incorporated

**67 Operation Petticoat** △
DIRECTOR Blake Edwards
SCENARIO Stanley Shapiro and Maurice Richlin
PHOTOGRAPHY Russell Harlan
EDITOR Ted J. Kent and Frank Gross
CAST Sherman (Cary Grant); Holden (Tony Curtis); Dolores (Joan O'Brien); Barbara (Dina Merrill); Molumphrey (Gene Evans); Tostin (Arthur O'Connell); Stovall (Richard Sargent); Major Edna Hayward (Virginia Gregg); Henderson (Robert F. Simon); Watson (Robert Gist); Hunkie (Gavin MacLeod); The Prophet (George Dunn); Harmon (Dick Crockett); Lt Claire Reid (Madlyn Rhue); Lt Ruth Colfax (Marion Ross); Ramon (Clarence E. Lung); Dooley (Frankie Darro); Fox (Tony Pastor

Jr.); Reiner (Robert Hoy); Kraus (Nicky Blair); Williams (John W. Morley); Crewman (William Bryant); Bowman (Bert Beyers); Fireman (Tony Corrado)
RUNNING TIME 124 minutes
RELEASE DATE 2 December 1959
PRODUCED BY Granart Company Productions

**68 The Grass Is Greener** ▽
DIRECTOR Stanley Donen
SCENARIO Hugh and Margaret Williams from their London play, *The Grass is Greener*
PHOTOGRAPHY Christopher Challis
EDITOR James Clark
CAST Victor Rhyall (Cary Grant); Hilary Rhyall (Deborah Kerr); Charles Delacro (Robert Mitchum); Hattie (Jean Simmons); Sellers (Moray Watson)
RUNNING TIME 104 minutes
RELEASE DATE January 1961
PRODUCED BY Grandon Productions Ltd

**69 That Touch of Mink** ▽
DIRECTOR Delbert Mann
SCENARIO Stanley Shapiro and Nate Monaster
PHOTOGRAPHY Russell Metty
EDITOR Ted J. Kent
CAST Philip Shayne (Cary Grant); Cathy Timberlake (Doris Day); Roger (Gig Young); Connie (Audrey Meadows); Dr Gruber (Alan Hewitt); Beasley (John Astin); Young Man (Richard Sargent); Short Man (Joey Faye); Showgirl (Laurie Mitchell); Mr Smith (John Fiedler); Hodges (Willard Sage); Dr Richardson

(Jack Livesey); Collins, chauffeur (John McKee); Millie (June Ericson); Mrs Golden (Laiola Wendorff)
RUNNING TIME 99 minutes
RELEASE DATE 18 July 1962
PRODUCED BY Granley Company-Arwin Productions Inc.-Nob Hill Productions, Inc.

**70 Charade** ▽
DIRECTOR Stanley Donen
SCENARIO Peter Stone, from the story *The Unsuspecting Wife* by Peter Stone, and Mark Behm
PHOTOGRAPHY Charles Lang
EDITOR James Clark
CAST Peter Joshua (Cary Grant); Regina 'Reggie' Lambert (Audrey Hepburn); Hamilton Bartholomew (Walter Matthau); Tex Penthollow (James Coburn); Herman Scobie (George Kennedy); Leopold Gideon (Ned Glass); Inspector Edouard Grandpierre (Jacques Marin); Felix (Paul Bonifas); Sylvie Gaudet (Dominique Minot); Jean-Louis Gaudet (Thomas Chelimsky)
RUNNING TIME 113 minutes
RELEASE DATE 25 December 1963
PRODUCED BY Universal-Stanley Donen

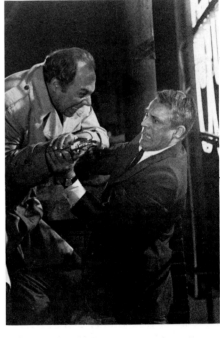

## 71 Father Goose ▷

DIRECTOR Ralph Nelson
SCENARIO Peter Stone and Frank Tarloff, from an unpublished story by S. H. Barnett entitled *A Place of Dragons*
PHOTOGRAPHY Charles Lang Jr.
EDITOR Ted J. Kent
CAST Walter Eckland (Cary Grant); Catherine Freneau (Leslie Caron); Comdr Frank Houghton (Trevor Howard); Lt Stebbins (Jack Good); Christine (Verina Greenlaw); Anne (Pip Sparke); Harriet (Jennifer Berrington); Elizabeth (Stephanie Berrington); Angelique (Lourelle Felsette); Dominique (Nicole Felsette); Jenny (Sharyl Locke); Submarine Captain (Simon Scott); Submarine Executive (John Napier); Radioman (Richard Lupino); Doctor (Alex Finlayson); Chaplain (Peter Forster); Navigator (Don Spruance); Helmsman (Ken Swofford)
RUNNING TIME 116 minutes
RELEASE DATE 24 December 1964
PRODUCED BY Granox Company Productions

## 72 Walk, Don't Run ▽

DIRECTOR Charles Walters
SCENARIO Sol Saks, based on a story by Robert Russell, and Frank Ross
PHOTOGRAPHY Harry Stradling
EDITOR Walter Thompson and James Wells
CAST William Rutland (Cary Grant); Christine Easton (Samantha Eggar); Steve Davis (Jim Hutton); Julius P. Haversack (John Standing); Aiko Kurawa (Miiko Taka); Yuri Andreyovitch (Ted Hartley); Dimitri (Ben Astar); Police Captain (George Takei); Mr Kurawa (Teru Shimada); Mrs Kurawa (Lois Kiuchi)
RUNNING TIME 114 minutes
RELEASE DATE 15 July 1966
PRODUCED BY Granley Company – a Sol C. Siegel Production

*Short Films and Guest Appearances*

### Singapore Sue (1932)
DIRECTOR Casey Robinson
SCENARIO written by Casey Robinson, with dialogue staged by Max E. Hayes
CAST Anna Chang; Cary Grant credited as Archie Leach

### Pirate Party on Catalina Isle (1936)
PRODUCED BY Louis Lewyn for Metro-Goldwyn-Mayer
CONTINUITY AND DIALOGUE Alexander van Dorn
CAST Chester Morris (Master of Ceremonies); with Marion Davies, Cary Grant, Virginia Bruce, John Gilbert, Lee Tracy, Errol Flynn, Lily Damita, Sid Silvers, Eddie Peabody, Leon Errol, Robert Armstrong and Charles (Buddy) Rogers and His Band as themselves
RUNNING TIME 20 minutes

### Topper Takes a Trip (1939) *Appearance*
DIRECTOR Norman Z. MacLeod
PRODUCED BY Milton Bren
Cary Grant was not available for this sequel to *Topper* (see main filmography). Short clips from the footage of the original featuring Grant were used as a story explanation.

### The Road to Victory (1944) *Appearance*
DIRECTOR LeRoy Prinz
CAST Bing Crosby, Cary Grant, Frank Sinatra, Charles Ruggles, Dennis Morgan, Irene Manning, Jack Carson, Jimmy Lydon, Olive Blakeney
RUNNING TIME 10 minutes
PRODUCED BY Warner Bros
Made for the War Activities Commission to boost the Fifth War Loan Drive.

### The Shining Future (1944) *Appearance*
DIRECTOR LeRoy Prinz
(Short)

### Without Reservations (1946) *Appearance*
DIRECTOR Mervyn LeRoy
PHOTOGRAPHY Milton Krasner
SCENARIO Andrew Solt
CAST Claudette Colbert (Kit); John Wayne (Rusty); with guest appearances by Cary Grant, Jack Benny, Louella Parsons
RUNNING TIME 107 minutes
PRODUCED BY Jesse L. Lasky Productions

### Polio and Communicable Diseases Hospital trailer (1940) *Appearance*
DIRECTOR Herman Hoffman
(Short)

### Ken Murray's Hollywood (1965) *Appearance*
DIRECTOR Ken Murray
Cary Grant appears in the Malibu party sequence.

### Elvis: That's the Way It Is (1970) *Appearance*
DIRECTOR Denis Sanders
SCENARIO Denis Sanders
PHOTOGRAPHY Lucien Ballard
EDITOR Henry Berman
RUNNING TIME 108 minutes
PRODUCED BY MGM
Cary Grant is among the celebrities attending the Elvis Summer Festival in Las Vegas in this documentary film.

### Once Upon a Time . . . Is Now (1977) *Voice only*
DIRECTOR Kevin Billington
American film made for television

# EPILOGUE 1986

IT SEEMED, SOMETIMES, THAT HE MIGHT ELUDE mortality itself – elude it as he had the infirmities, inanities and indignities of octagenarianism – so chipper had he seemed as he went about his cheerful business in his last three years. Indeed, if anything, Cary Grant went more in public during this period than he had at any point since his retirement from the screen. He had added to his customary round of business activities, the race track and the ballpark, more appearances at charitable and ceremonial occasions than had been his previous wont. And he had devised a one-man show which he took about on the lecture circuit. In it, he projected clips from his films and answered – or appeared to answer – questions from the audience about his life and work.

In fact, these programmes of his were also exercises in the art of elusiveness, for by all accounts he revealed almost nothing except charm in response to the tactful (not to say worshipful) questions that were put to him. So artfully did he combine wit with modesty in his remarks that it generally did not occur to his questioners that he had really said nothing substantial – until, perhaps, they were on the road home.

But, of course, charm was everything by that time. It was what they expected of him, desperately wanted from him, *needed* from him in this increasingly charmless era. For everywhere there were people and publications offering them the lowdown, the scoop, the dirt on everything and everybody. In these circumstances, it was wonderfully reassuring to find oneself in the presence of a man who had not the slightest need or desire to elevate himself by gossiping about friends and colleagues of the past, or by turning his autobiography into melodrama or morality play. And to see this edifying performance, by a man still light on his feet and agile of mind, was a lesson in grace and gallantry not soon to be forgotten.

It was, of course, to repeat this performance that Cary Grant came at last to the unlikely venue of his demise, Davenport, Iowa, where he suffered a stroke on Saturday 29 November 1986, dying later that evening. By suddenly slipping away as he did, in a remote corner of the world, at a moment when the Sunday papers had been safely put to bed, he did what he could to diminish the obituary orgy that he surely knew would attend his passing. Even in one's saddened condition, when the news of his death was belatedly communicated (by radio reporters requesting phone interviews with a biographer late the next morning) one could not help but reflect that he had somehow contrived to die as he had lived – in a manner that as far as possible prevented strangers from laying clumsy hands on his image. The subsequent news that he had requested no funeral or memorial service deepened one's appreciation of Cary Grant's sense of the fitness of things.

Still, the press, as usual, did its best to go on misleading its public – and Grant's – about the nature of his public persona and his achievement as an actor. Charm, charm, charm: that was all that it could seem to talk about as it stretched the story for all it was worth. 'A class act,' television commentators kept saying, with the pleased air of people making a profound social comment, the implication being that there had been few enough of *those* in vulgar Hollywood.

Perhaps the writers of the appraisals and bios and memoirs of meaningless encounters with Grant were too young to recall the great movies of his younger manhood; perhaps all they had to go on was the quick-silver celebrity images of the later years, from which Grant had finally refined all the autobiographical impurities which had enlivened the performances of the late Thirties and early Forties. Perhaps the star had done his work all too well in his later years, insisting so firmly on his own weightlessness that people refused to believe the evidence of their own eyes when they encountered the subtleties and ambiguities of, say, *Notorious* or *Suspicion, His Girl Friday* or

*The Philadelphia Story.* After all, Grant did frequently tell people that his own favorite among his films was *Indiscreet*.

Given these maunderings, and given the sure and certain knowledge that the ever-simplifying, ever-sentimentalising media now have the power to blunt all attempts at critical distinctions, one's previously expressed confidence that posterity would inevitably find the essence of the man not in the delicious deviousness with which he lived his later life, but in the truthfulness of his earlier art, is somewhat shaken. But history – even movie history – is too important a matter to be left to Yuppie journalism. So, for the record, one must insist on this point: the subject of his greatest films, his greatest work, was not charm, but its fragile and illusionary nature in a world where brutality often masquerades as farce and romance is often the disguise of deviousness and manipulation. That, in later years, he either chose not to acknowledge what he had been doing or could not recognise what he had so brilliantly accomplished, was his business – and it was pleasant to go along with that devious gag. Now that he is gone, however, and his feelings cannot be hurt by our attempts to make him own up to his dark side, those of us who loved his art have an obligation to insist that it was both real and magically subtle – and of a higher value than the celebrity image whose passing was so noisily mourned in the early winter of 1986.

Acknowledgements

The following illustrations appear by the kind permission of:

Keystone Press: p.23 (top), 159 (bottom)
Mander and Mitchenson: p.25
Museum of Modern Art: p.29, 81 (middle), 156 (top)
Popperfoto: p.22 (left), 47 (right), 118, 126
Rex Features: p.23 (bottom)
UPI: p.7 (left), 11, 18, 21, (top left), 138, 158, 172/173

The publishers acknowledge with thanks the co-operation of the following:

The Bison Archives, Columbia, MGM, Paramount, RKO, Twentieth Century Fox, Universal Pictures.